WEDDINGS UNFILTERED

The no bullsh*t wedding-planning guide

WEDDINGS UNFILTERED

The no bullsh*t wedding-planning guide

Jessica Sclafini

With Special Thanks to Erin Waszak

Cover Design: Mike Mangione

Editor: Michele Kerulis

ISBN: 978-0-692-91568-4

www.weddings-unfiltered.com

Dad you taught me to be strong, confident, and independent; to be a free thinker and problem solver. You taught me the art of negotiation and how to make a deal...because there is always a deal to be made. You taught me the importance of friends and family and of loyalty, even when you have your differences. You taught me about motivation, failure and success, and determination and hard work. You taught me to love and appreciate music, even though we usually had different ideas of what music was. Most importantly, you taught me invaluable lessons about life and I apply your extreme words of wisdom daily. You were my best friend, my biggest fan, my biggest critic, and my biggest motivator.

I love you and miss you every single day.

Acknowledgements

I would first and foremost like to thank Erin Waszak for being a friend, a sounding board, and a fabulous wedding planning consultant. Without you, many of these crazy stories would not have come to life.

Michele Kerulis, my editor, your strength, and determination is inspiring. You brought this idea to realization and I am beyond grateful to know you as a person and consider you a friend.

Mike Mangione, thank you for making my vision for a book cover a reality.

Amy Rita, thank you for formatting the entire book and doing the margins and fonts and bleed…whatever the hell that even means!

To the hundreds of brides, grooms, and vendors that I have met along the way, none of this would be possible without any of you. Thank you for teaching me the extremely necessary skills of patience and problem solving. You have taught me to act as a therapist at times, and have enabled me to understand the meaning of nervous wreck (although everything always seemed to work out!). Finally, thank you for providing me years of pure entertainment!

Vince, I thank you for your support during these last three years. You calmed every storm that I encountered and opened my eyes to a deeper understanding of myself and others around me. I miss you so much.

Thank you to my friends and family for dealing with me and all of my crazy projects that I come up with daily. You have all helped me in one way or another by supporting me, pushing me, telling me when I'm being an asshole, picking me up when I stumble time and time again, and for truly loving me. You've been my backbone throughout so much of my life. I appreciate you all more than you'll ever know. Some people I love the most that I'd like to mention: mom, Jennifer, Frank, and Carla for having my back always.

Vikki- you are my voice of reason. Bridget- you're just my person. Piera- you are my oldest and dearest friend...the things we've been through together. Rebecca- you are my travel buddy and my forever partner in crime. Carrie- you are my world problem solving partner...on Saturdays...and the best researcher I know. Amanda- my boss- ha! You are just a damn good friend to me and I appreciate it more than I can put in words.

Last but not least, thank you to two of my favorite people: Jack and Brooke for teaching me something new every day and reminding me how innocent and pure life can be.

Table of Contents

Introduction

Here comes the happy couple! God help us.

There comes a time in our lives when every single one of us has been affected by a wedding. Whether it's your mother, father, brother, sister, friend, or even foe, we have all been affected by a wedding. Me included. I'm a wedding planner. Like a real one, not a "I was in a wedding once so now I can easily do this for other people" kind of wedding planner. I have made a wonderful living as a wedding planner for over 10 years. With that said, I have seen it all, done it all, read it all, lived it all. The bottom line everyone involved in a wedding has gotten to the point where we take a step back and think to ourselves *WTF?* This is *one* day of their lives—*only one*. One single day that many brides have described as a blur—*a blur*! You might ask yourself, how did I not know my best friend (sibling, granddaughter, or whomever) was bat-shit crazy (temporarily)! How did I also not know she had horrible taste. . . in everything (hopefully not in the fiancée; if so, we usually just go with it). We have all seen the television shows that make being totally insane, breaking the bank, and demanding a bigger and better, well, everything, is somehow acceptable. The entertainment industry even kind of glamorizes it. I can assure you nothing about this type of behavior is glamorous—nothing. It's time to finally come clean and shout out what every single person has most likely thought at one point or another but would *never* dare say to the blushing bride or groom! Buckle up friends, it's about to go down.

Planning a wedding should be a fun experience; however, it will most likely be immensely overwhelming and stressful. You have a million thoughts running through your head. The fairy tale you've always dreamed of is about to come true. That is, until you look at the price tag and all of a sudden, your dreams come to a screeching halt and reality sets in. Weddings are unbelievably expensive! It's time to prioritize and get organized. That's where I can help.

So, what sets this book apart from the rest?

You're all probably thinking you can search any topic and get information on the Internet. Yes, you can and about a million sites will pop-up on a million things that you didn't even know existed. That sounds easy...to *no one*. I have condensed everything you need and should want to know to get you started with the planning process in this little, easy to read book.

The so-called advice websites somehow manage to wrap-up all the wedding planning in a neat, perfect little package, complete with a ribbon tied around it. That, my friends, is very deceiving. Planning a wedding is fricken hard! It takes time, organization, and help from people who know what they're doing. I am not here to sugar coat anything and pretend it's all perfect because it's not. Nothing is perfect! (Although we try very *very* hard as planners to make weddings as perfect as possible with the happy couple being none the wiser.)

I love observing behavior from all types of clients, and feel the need to put an end to the ridiculous notion that because you are getting married, you rule the world. Just stop it! Weddings are typically based on emotion without considering logic. Let's get over the emotion and get with the realism of the wedding planning. There will be triumphs and there will be tragedies. Don't let the perceived tragedies distract from the real reason you are getting married.

This is a little handbook about weddings seen through the eyes of a wedding planner who has also been a bridesmaid in many weddings. This book will discuss the harsh realities of these triumphs and tragedies my clients and friends have experienced through their amazing journeys while still landing on their feet for their special day. I will help you through the stress of preparing for your big day, all while exploiting the absurdities, yet painful truths, with a side of some very useful tips, of wedding planning. I've also incorporated personal stories for a few reasons. I feel such stories will help not only put things into perspective but also acknowledge that everyone goes through the same things you are, and honestly, I just can't make this shit up.

To all of my same sex engaged couples, I stopped wedding planning before your union became legal. Congratulations to you all! I really missed the boat on this one.

CHAPTER 1
Let's get real!

Before we get started on the timeline from getting engaged to getting you down the aisle, let's discuss some pretty important issues. Basically, how we'd like to conduct ourselves during the planning process and what sort of expectations we can set forth.

First, *This. Is. One. Day.* You don't get to treat people poorly because you have a ring on your finger. Second, it is important to normalize the fact that all brides experience a spectrum of emotions from complete excitement to utter despair. Just know that you are not alone and when you become overwhelmed with emotion please take a minute, breathe, and refocus. You will get through this and you will be great. So, grab your highlighter, a glass of wine, settle into a cozy spot and let's work together ... all while keeping your Xanax at a safe distance.

Now, before we begin with the timeline from the moment you become engaged leading up to the "I do's," I want to share with you what I've learned through my 10-plus years of experience working with hundreds of couples. You read that right—hundreds—Oh, the stories I'm going to tell you!

Being engaged is probably one of the happiest and most exciting times of one's life, but as mentioned before, it can also be extremely overwhelming and stressful. You will most likely experience highs and lows, laughter and tears, doubts and a bit of fear, mixed with crossed arms over your chest and angry glares. That's just all while working on the seating chart. The point is, throughout this entire journey on which you are about to embark, it is critical that you remember my two favorite words: One Day. Understanding the meaning of those two simple words can help put the upcoming year into perspective. It is also extremely crucial that you set forth realistic expectations for others, and more importantly, for you and your fiancé.

Brace yourselves my friends. The cold hard fact is no one cares about your wedding as much as you. There—I said it!

There are, however, a few exceptions to this reality. For instance, your parents may be just as excited for these nuptials. (Then again, their excitement could quite possibly be for all the wrong reasons, like hosting the wedding of their own dreams!). Surely, your future in-laws will share in your excitement, or not. Your grandparents may also be just as enthused. (Well, that depends on how many weddings they've attended of other grandchildren.) And maybe, hopefully, your fiancé will be just as excited.

Of course, your siblings and friends will be genuinely happy for you and just as excited, especially if they like your future spouse. However, this does not mean the lives of everyone mentioned above should stop or be put on hold for the next year while you plan your pending nuptials. Please note, I am not saying this to be mean or downplay the excitement of your engagement. I am saying this as a reminder so that you don't have any unrealistic expectations of people and their actions.

Here's another tiny blow. And this may come as a surprise to you, but you are actually not the first person to get married. What?! I know! It's crazy! Remember, none of us deserve anything. We should appreciate everything people do for us. Do not set yourself up for disappointment because people are not reacting the way you expected them to. Friends and family will be there for you and do the best they can in helping, but life does go on for everyone. Have respect. Have realistic expectations. But, most importantly, have fun!

Let's talk about expectations of everyone that will be involved in making your wedding day special.

Weddings result in the union of two people that binds them together in life and love. With this in mind, use your wedding planning time as practice in working together as a couple. Throughout many parts of this book when I write "you" I am referring to you as a couple, not just you as the bride. With this said, remember to appreciate those who help you with the planning process and do not assign unrealistic expectations.

EXPECTATIONS OF THE GROOM

Really? Isn't proposing enough of an expectation? While I'm kind of kidding, let's be real here. This is not something the average guy has dreamed about his entire life. He is most likely, at some point, going to be afraid of you and will just do whatever will make you happy. And that is a good thing . . . to a point.

I've seen three types of grooms: The Nightmare, The Dream, and The Reality.

The Nightmare Groomzilla. This type of groom exists and is no joke. It is very rare that this happens, but when it does, I find myself questioning so many things. Don't get me wrong, I am all about groom participation, but it's almost like groomzillas try to dominate the situation. I often find myself thinking, "Is this really someone you want to marry?" I think you can tell the kind of relationship people have based on the wedding-planning journey. I know it sounds ridiculous, but it's interesting to watch how couples interact with one another and handle certain situations as the planning progresses. If a groom is extremely controlling and doesn't let one single detail slip through his fingers, is it like looking into the future? I'll just leave that there.

The Dream Groom. This is the groom who is genuinely happy to be involved in helping plan the wedding. You two work as partners in making decisions and making the wedding about the two of you. He will gladly follow your lead, express his opinions, and even come-up with ways to make things better. If this is your groom, be extremely grateful he put a ring on it.

The Reality Groom. The "just tell me when and where groom" most likely doesn't really care about the small or big details of your wedding except maybe for the music choice and the bar option. The Reality Groom will often pretend to have an opinion, but will ultimately agree with you and go with whatever you decide. This is the person who gets dragged to every single appointment and sits and pretends to listen because he feels he has to. Chances are, he is thinking about a million other things he'd rather be doing . . . especially during the weekends, like football, drinking beer, cleaning out the garage, drinking beer, lying on the couch, drinking beer, did I mention football? Many brides look at this and think, "At least he came with me, even though he is frustrating me because he really isn't giving his opinion or even listening." This doesn't mean he doesn't care about you. He just isn't sweating the small stuff or any of the stuff actually. This is OK. He wants you to have your version of a dream wedding and will stand by your side while you achieve it. Unless you start searching the Internet for things like "dove release," he most likely will not chime-in with his opinion. It's not a bad thing. If you know this is your groom, do not expect him to attend every appointment with you and all of a sudden ask a ton of questions and become excited when you find the perfect frame to put your wedding invitation in for the place-card table. Don't get frustrated with him because he doesn't have an opinion about every single detail.

Instead of expecting your groom to attend, especially if you know he doesn't want to be there, bring your girlfriends or mother and mother-in-law to these appointments. You want someone who will get excited about the menu, the linen selections, as well as the mini-rhinestone picture frames that'll be perfect for the table numbers. Save yourself the arguments as it will be more fun this way and you can fill him in later.

*Side note: Be aware of planning a wedding during your fiancé's favorite sports season and keep these things in mind if you are not a big sports fan. Is he a football fan? If so, then good luck making vendor appointments around fantasy football drafts. Above all else, don't plan your wedding Super Bowl weekend. You may even be coaxed into wearing matching football jerseys as you walk into your reception.

EXPECTATIONS OF PARENTS

If you are relying or expecting parents to pay for the entire wedding, also expect them to have a very loud opinion about everything. Rightfully so, *right*? This includes the ceremony and reception site(s), the dress, the menu, the guest list, and of course this will instigate the DJ versus band debate.

Tradition has taught us that the parents of the bride pays for the wedding and the parents of the groom pay for the rehearsal dinner. If this is the case for your wedding, that is fantastic. Be grateful. Look at this gesture as more of a gift than an entitlement. Not all families can afford to do this. Despite tradition, this is really no longer the norm. With that said, parents paying can sometimes have the "overrule" status of how the wedding is finalized. If you are young and can't afford a wedding, then you are very lucky to have parents who can. If you are in your 30s or 40s with a steady income, consider contributing.

~PERSONAL STORY~

The "Later Bitches" Bride

I worked with a bride once whose parents were paying for the entire wedding, which was awesome, except for the fact that it was nothing she wanted. She was a simple gal wanting a simple but beautiful destination wedding. Her mother wanted the complete opposite. An over the top, extravagant, let's invite everyone you've ever met since third grade and cover everything in crystals kind of mom. At the beginning of the planning process they'd butt heads, and finally my bride grew silent and uninvolved. We set-up a meeting, which the bride then cancelled on a whim. (Eventually, she rescheduled.)

We needed to reschedule that meeting because she and her future husband decided that planning a wedding that wasn't theirs wasn't worth it. They got married in a court house then flew to Mexico for a weekend wedding getaway. They ultimately had the intimate beach wedding they wanted. Her mother was obviously not thrilled, but she eventually got over it. *I think?*

Regardless of who is involved and how your wedding will be funded, don't settle for your special day being dictated by anyone else besides you and your fiancé. It's your day and no one else's. Compromise, be respectful of opinions, but most importantly make it your own.

And mother of the brides and grooms, learn from this story. Don't be momzillas. It's embarrassing. Would you rather push your son or daughter away and risk not even being involved, or should you take a back seat and let them make decisions regarding their wedding. Maybe they'll even value your opinion more when they ask for help and you might wind-up having a fun time planning together. What a concept!

EXPECTATIONS OF THE ACTUAL DAY

No day is perfect and your wedding day will be no exception. This is not a reason to panic. Inevitably, something *will* go wrong on your special day. However, it is up to you to set the tone of the day. If you are stressed or unhappy about something, it will reflect and in turn can result in others around you feeling the same way. No one knows the details of your wedding, so it really doesn't matter if something is missing. In fact, your caterer could even serve the wrong dish, but no one will know. You need to stay calm and relaxed, and remember what this day is really about. If it's about the meal, the flowers or the cake, you should probably rethink the marriage altogether. The only thing you really need for this day to be a success is both of you showing up (fingers crossed). That's it. Pretty simple, don't ya think?

News Flash: You *cannot* control Mother Nature. If you live in a region that has an unpredictable climate and you are considering an outdoor wedding, be aware that your special day can be destroyed due to potential and unexpected weather patterns. If this is something you have dreamed of your entire life, then I suggest a destination wedding. At the very least, be sure you have a plan B.

While working as a wedding planner in Chicago, I have seen far too many brides obsessed with checking the weather forecast. *Seriously?* Anyone that lives in such climates should be well aware that the day can start off being beautifully sunny with a slight cool breeze blowing. Within 20 minutes, literally 20 minutes, temperatures can drop by at least 30 degrees and no umbrella will save you or your hair for the monsoon that is about to take place.

In one day. My point, you will *never* know what Mother Nature has in store for you. Instead of driving yourself crazy because your ceremony is outside, please for the love of God, make sure that there are alternative choices to moving the ceremony inside. Your best bet is to have an indoor ceremony with a lovely terrace where guests can enjoy cocktails and hors d'oeuvres, weather permitting, of course.

~PERSONAL STORY~
THE IVY BRIDE

I was a guest at a wedding where the bride chose her venue based on the unique outdoor space that was surrounded by buildings covered in ivy. It looked like a beautifully landscaped park in the middle of the city. It was absolutely stunning. The idea was that all guests would enjoy the cocktail hour in the ivy covered outdoor space, return inside for dinner, and continue the evening with the option to enjoy both the indoor and outdoor spaces. Well, this may come as a huge surprise, but it rained the entire day. I don't mean a little drizzle. I'm talking monsoon like weather with strong winds that blew the rain sideways. Clearly, the flooded outdoor space was just not going to work. Instead of having a plan B (*why would you?*) all guests were crammed into what I can only describe as a basement for cocktails and then brought upstairs for the remainder of the reception. The lighting guy was able to project twigs and trees on the walls, and it looked like we were outside, which was really cool, actually. But, unfortunately the happy couple never got to actually enjoy the reason they booked the venue in the first place.

I can't stress this enough: something will go wrong on your wedding day. It will usually be something minor, but something will happen. So please take comfort in knowing that this happens at every wedding and it gets taken care of, most of the time without the bride even realizing the problem. Again, it's usually minor so don't freak out.

DO YOU KNOW THE WEDDING LINGO?

Let's get acquainted with some popular wedding terms. Acronyms are often used. This glossary will help you understand what the hell everyone is talking about.

1. Banquet captain - Your point of contact during the reception after your event manager has completed his/her duties for the evening.

2. Banquet Event Order (BEO) – Venue employees and vendors refer to this document on the day of the wedding. It includes the timeline, menu, and all the other important specifics. . . Be sure every single detail discussed with your venue or caterer is included in your BEO.

3. Best Man (BM) - The Best Man is traditionally assigned by the groom. His role includes planning the bachelor party and is the groom's right-hand man on the wedding day.

4. Bridal Room/Suite – The bridal party can safely store personal items in this private room at the ceremony and/or reception.

5. Bustle - Buttoning or hooking the back of a wedding dress to hold up the train.

6. Charger - Large decorative plate placed under dinner plate to add color or texture.

7. Chivari Chairs - Upgraded wooden framed chairs that usually have a seat cushion.

8. Cabaret Tables - Short tables with 2 - 4 chairs generally used to provide seating in a cocktail style setting.

9. Day of Coordinator (DOC) - A person who is hired to help you coordinate and finalize all specific details for your wedding day.

10. Do It Yourself (DIY) - I kinda feel this is self-explanatory. DIY is something that you do on your own, by yourself. Get it?

11. Event Manager - Your point of contact at your wedding venue. This person will help plan all details of the wedding reception and/or ceremony if you choose to have it on site.

12. Food and Beverage (F & B) - Shorthand for the food and beverage served at your wedding.

13. Father of the Bride (FOB) - The man the bride considers to be her father or father figure.

14. Father of the Groom (FOB) - The man the groom calls dad.

15. High-boy/High-top - Tall tables used in a cocktail setting to provide a gathering space while standing.

16.   Lapel/Lavalier   Microphone - A   small microphone, usually used during the ceremony, which can be clipped onto an article of clothing.

17.   Mother of the Bride (MOB) - The woman the bride considers to be her mother or mother figure.

18.   Mother of the Groom (MOG) - The woman the groom calls mom.

19.   Maid of Honor (not married) Matron of Honor (married) - The maid of honor is traditionally assigned by the bride. She is responsible for putting up with the bride's crap, planning the bachelorette party, and assisting the family with planning the shower.

20.   Minimum Revenue - The amount of money you are required to spend in food and beverage before tax and gratuity.

21.   Overlay - An overlay is an additional linen piece that lies over the tablecloth, covering the top of the table and slightly around the sides. This is typically used to add a pop of color or shimmer to your tables.

22.   Risers - A low platform on a stage or in an auditorium used to give greater prominence to a speaker or performer.

23.   Skirting - The draping of a tablecloth to make it look more formal and elegant.

24. Sweet Table - A table at the reception that offers a variety of desserts in addition to the dessert served during your meal.

25. Sweetheart Table - A table set up at the reception for just you and your husband to sit at during dinner as opposed to a head table.

26. Table Runner - Cut of fabric, usually 1 foot in width, placed across the table linen to add a hint of color.

27. Tablescape - Another name for a table arrangement or centerpiece when one consists of multiple components like florals and candles.

28. Wedding Planner - Person who puts up with way too much shit to make sure your special day is one to remember.

So, now that we're prepped and ready--Let's do this!

Chapter 2

AAAHHH! *You're engaged! Holy crap.* Now What?

12 Months out

He finally popped the question and you said yes! Once the cloud you're floating on dissipates and you've shown off your bling to every single person on the planet, while still admiring the sparkle in the side view mirror as you drive, it's time to start the planning. The first tip is to get organized. The best way to stay organized is to work within a timeline from the moment you get engaged until the day you walk down the aisle. Let's work with a timeline of one year.

WEDDING VISION

Creating a wedding vision is the first step in determining how to move forward with your planning. What does your dream wedding look like? Understanding the overall look and feel you are trying to achieve will help determine so many other important details like guest count, date of the wedding, and ultimately your budget. Do you envision a Traditional Glam Wedding? A Destination Wedding? A Daytime lunch or brunch? A Unique Site? I've listed examples of several different types of weddings to help you figure out your own vision.

Traditional Glam Wedding - A traditional glam wedding can hold any amount of people. This is your standard wedding reception. It will most commonly be held in a banquet hall at a hotel, or country club. These sites will offer a variety of room sizes that will accommodate a minimum of about 75 people and can go up to a few hundred. This type of wedding will be an evening reception and carry all the usual bells and whistles from the ceremony to the reception which will include a 3-5 course seated meal. If you're Italian or Greek, tack on about 3 more additional courses and a sweet table. Many of us have attended this type of event.

Destination Wedding - The destination wedding is a smaller, more intimate setting. Guests join you at a destination that is away from where the couple lives. Think tropical beach! This is one of my personal favorites. Not only do you have your closest family and friends with you, you simultaneously have the relaxation of being on vacation. I don't know about you, but the second I'm on vacation, I am content and ready to enjoy my time. You will of course have details to work out, as it is your wedding after all, but I can't think of a better way to work them out than while sipping on a tropical cocktail and feeling the sunlight on my face (can you tell I'm from Chicago and currently battling the never-ending winter?).

You can make it a weekend long event in the sun and on a beach! Start with a welcome dinner, a fun day of activities (which can consist of a day in the sun at the pool or beach if you'd like), followed by a rehearsal dinner, the actual wedding day, and maybe a brunch the morning after. Remember, this is you, your fiancée, and your closest friends and family all on vacation enjoying each other's company! What a great way to start your life together. Keep in mind that most guests will make your wedding a mini vacation for themselves.

With that said, if you and your new spouse are planning on the honeymoon to begin right after the wedding and you don't change resorts or locations you'll often run into family and friends. And let's be honest, they all know what you're doing at night. (cue porn music . . . I'll spell it out for you *bow chicka bow wow*). However, it can be so fun to have all of your guests with you to re-experience the night and share stories of things you might have missed during a post-wedding night brunch. After a day or two, you might be family and friended out and simply exhausted. You might just want to relax with your new husband and take in everything that has just happened. Just as you're dozing off in the beautiful sun at a beautiful resort thinking of your magically perfect night - BAM here comes Aunt Mil in her never should be seen in public bikini, oversized beach hat, and sunglasses (You automatically think: "Was she wearing this 5 days ago? Why didn't it bother me then?"), asking when the two of you are going to have a baby. You have now been married for a total of five minutes.

Also, know the marital laws of the country where you plan to wed. Most often couples get married in the U.S. before their actual destination wedding to ensure that they are legally married. You don't want to get married in another country and come back only to find out you're not actually legally married. Oops, that would suck.

Cocktail and Heavy Hors d'oeuvres Wedding - This can be done anywhere you choose. It consists of an open bar and heavy hors d'oeuvres. You want to have 10-12 pieces of food per person. You can have them passed around the room (butlered) or set up buffet style or stations. You usually don't provide seating for all guests so there is no seating chart to worry about. *Huge Bonus!*

I suggest combining regular tables with high tops. This creates more of a mingling atmosphere. Try to reserve a few tables for elderly guests such as grandparents and guests with physical limitations.

Keep in mind food will last longer if you provide a combination of passed and displayed hors d oeuvres. If you put it all out there in hopes people will ration for themselves, guess what? They won't and it'll be gone. You know the rule . . . if you build it, they will come . . . and they will come hungry . . . with take home containers . . . or really big purses. Ah, grandparents.

Lunch/Brunch Wedding - A lunch brunch wedding will be more cost efficient than the other types of weddings mentioned in this section given it will be during the day. You will have lower pricing so you can have as many or as little guests as you'd like. This is something fun and different! You can serve your favorite brunch selections from waffles and crepes to a carving station and salad. I suggest having a bloody mary or mimosa bar . . . or both! You don't have to offer a full on open bar - after all, you're probably hosting this mid-day. You can enjoy a wonderful day with all of your guests and have the entire evening free to keep the party going or run far away from everyone because at this point they are all driving you crazy! It's completely up to you.

Unique Site Wedding - A unique site wedding includes barns, mansions, museums, libraries, city lofts, amazing restaurants, and more. Depending on the venue, this may be the most expensive choice given the fact that many, if not all, of these venues will require you to provide everything from chairs and place settings; decor and accents; and everything in between. There are a lot of event design companies that provide one stop shopping. While using event designers is the easiest option, it may not be the most cost efficient.

There are some really cool spaces out there to hold weddings. I think this option is for the creative types who have a complete vision of what they want and the money to get it. However, if you are looking for an intimate and unique venue that won't bust your budget, try one of your favorite restaurants. Restaurants often have a private room that can hold at least 30 people and you are guaranteed to get a great meal and service for you and your guests.

BUDGET

Plan a budget! Setting a budget and sticking to it is the single most important thing you can do for yourself and your future (and perhaps a little bit of your sanity!). Will you be receiving financial help from parents, grandparents, and future in-laws, or are you and your future spouse solely responsible for the cost of the wedding? Is spending every penny ever given or earned worth it on one day? Is it important to you to have a nest egg? A down payment on a house? A dream vacation or honeymoon? This is one day of your life, people. Remember that. *One. Day. Of. Your. Life.* Yes ladies, this is one day of your life. Repeat that, this is one day of your life. . . say it over and over, make it your mantra but don't forget it. (This sentence will be repeated many times throughout this book)

The good news is that no matter what the budget is, you can still have the wedding of your dreams by finding less expensive alternatives to some insanely expensive options. (Which we'll get to in a bit). You might not ride up into the parking lot of your wedding venue in some car with a name no one can even pronounce. Heads up, you're not a celeb. Paparazzi is not all over your wedding. Let the dream die. . . because it's ridiculous.0

This is a good start to the budget planning. It will inevitably change to fit your needs and wants (e.g. the rings), but it provides a great guideline. It is important to discuss with your partner what seems most important and where you are willing to compromise. You may not even want all of the things on the list above. If not, save the money or put it toward something more meaningful to you. *Prioritize!*

Something that is extremely important to understand and the most common misconception is that you will make back the money you have spent in wedding gifts from your guests. It just doesn't work that way. If you don't have the money to pay for it, do not do it!! In our minds, our guests will at the very least cover the cost of their plates. The problem is people just don't know the cost of your meal and how expensive it is. When I worked at a banquet hall, I used to have wedding guests call and ask for a rough estimate of what the meal cost. I appreciated their effort.

I realize you might want to pay for your wedding on a credit card to get the miles or earn cash back, but have that cash to pay it off every month. DO NOT rely on those guests' cards to pay off all of your debt. You'll be paying it off for years to come. Plus interest. That is a bad start to your happily ever after. This is what I recommend for a wedding budget breakdown:

Reception Venue food beverage - 50%

Attire - 10%

Flowers and Décor - 10%

Music - 10%

Photography - 10%

Favors and gifts - 2%

Ceremony - 2%

Stationery - 2%

Wedding Rings - 2%

Transportation - 1%

Additional Gratuities or just for a little cushion - 1%

Gratuity - Additional Gratuity will be discussed in a later chapter and can change depending on your experience with vendors. Gratuity is something to keep in mind when planning your budget.

Here is an example of a wedding budget with dollar values used to demonstrate percentage allocations. It is very important to keep in mind these numbers are used just for a point of reference. It does NOT mean this will be the cost of your wedding. For instance, typically a suburban wedding will be less expensive than a city wedding. There are many individual factors that will affect the cost of your wedding. To keep it simple for our mathematically challenged friends, such as myself, let's say an average wedding for 100 people at a standard banquet hall is roughly $25,000.00.

The breakdown would be as follows:

Reception Venue/food/beverage- $12,500.00

Attire- $2,500.00

Flowers and Decor- $2,500.00

Music- $2,500.00

Photography- $2,500.00

Favors and gifts- $500.00

Ceremony- $500.00

Stationary- $500.00

Wedding rings- $500.00- UH…*hmmm..kinda bs!*

Transportation- $250.00

Additional Gratuities or just for a little cushion- $250.00

Also, I understand not everyone stays within their budget because things just come up. However, either include that little cushion room for the unexpected, or think about that one thing you might not need. I've seen way too many couples toward the end of their planning say, "Who cares!" and start throwing their money around like it's no big deal because they become frustrated and are "so over it." **Don't** do this!!! Spend your money wisely and cautiously. It may sound ridiculous that people would do this, but they do. Be aware, you'll thank me in the end.

WEDDING PLANNER: TO HIRE OR NOT TO HIRE?

This is a good time to start thinking about hiring a wedding planner. The two kinds of planners are full service wedding planner and the day of coordinator. Both can help you reduce stress on your big day.

The first option is a full-service wedding planner (think J-LO in *The Wedding Planner* . . . hopefully with a different outcome for you) who will take charge of your entire wedding. This is for the couple who has a hefty budget and wants help making every major decision. The wedding planner will help pick out flowers, linens, music, the menu (which I never understood why the planner would ever come to the tasting- don't the bride and groom know what they like to eat?), and plan everything in between.

The cost of hiring a wedding planner will fluctuate depending on if your planner is an independent contractor or employed by an event planning company. Some planners charge hourly, some charge based on a percentage of your total budget, and others charge package rates. A planner who is more experienced will have higher rates.

The second option is a Day of Coordinator (DOC). A DOC will be far less expensive than full service wedding planner and will guide you in the final months of planning to ensure that the actual day runs smoothly. The DOC will meet with you a couple of months before the wedding to help plan the timeline and gather all vendor contact information. Most will be with you at your rehearsal, ceremony, and of course reception site the day of the wedding to set up the room and extinguish any small fires that will inevitably arise throughout the day. Day of Coordinators charge hourly or will offer packages.

Regardless of which type of planner you choose, it is important to meet with this person one-on-one and see if you work well together. Your planner will spend a lot of time with you and help you with very personal details (yes, I have held brides' dresses while they peed, got under their dresses to get them bustled before the reception, was a makeshift hairdresser and seamstress if need be. The list is endless.) so you want to be comfortable around her.

On a side note, for brides who do plan to hire wedding planners, please listen to them. They will help you. They know a lot of people in the industry and will most likely be able to negotiate deals or guide you in the right direction. If you think you know better than someone who has made a career out of this and plans weddings daily, attending far, far too many to count, please, do us a favor and do not hire us. Hire the girl that has planned her own wedding, thought it was super fun, and is now calling herself a wedding planner - which isn't insulting at all. Also please keep in mind, we are wedding planners, not florists, bakers, or musicians. There are a lot of moving parts to a wedding that must all come together - it is our job to make sure other vendors show up and scramble to figure out a solution if they don't. So know we are working very hard to make your dream a reality.

WEDDING DATE AND TIME

Now that you know what type of wedding you want and what sort of budget you have, it's time to pick a date. Many people plan about a year out, so if there is a particular date that means something to you, or if you have your eye on a certain venue and or band that you *must have,* book it now! Be aware of festivals, concerts, tradeshows, and other potentially conflictual events that fall on your desired date. Before you lock in a date, do your research and know what's going on in your area around that date. Did you just book a venue next to a stadium and there's a game that weekend? Did you lock in a date that turned out to be Easter or Passover that year? Put some thought into your date and time to avoid these conflicts.

When planning the time of year, there are some things to take into consideration. Whether you are looking at a banquet hall, golf course, or hotel, off season pricing will be offered. Off season generally runs from November through March with major holidays, like New Years, are excluded. You can usually get discounted pricing on Saturdays during these off months. However, regardless of the month, there is always a discount for Friday and Sunday weddings. (Again, holiday weekends, Memorial Day, Labor Day not included). If you book over a year out, ask to lock in your current price as they most likely will change the next year. More information about obtaining discounts will be discussed in each "budget friendly tip" section.

GUEST LIST

You want to have a tentative guest list planned because the first question a reception site will ask is what date do you have in mind and second how many people are you anticipating? This is often difficult because it will be hard to determine how many people you can afford to invite without knowing the price per person. The best way to get started is simply make a list of the bride's family with the help of your parents, while the groom makes a list of his own with the help of his. Then add your friends to the list and see where you're at. Are you at 75 or 500?

Once you have created the first draft of your guest list you can multiply the number of guests' times the cost per person and see what the total is. If this number is way out of your price range it is time to revise. It's also a good idea to have a secondary list, your B list, that consists of people you aren't actually sure are your real friends. Just because you were friends when you were eight and played in the park every day and are linked on social media does not mean that person needs a wedding invitation.

One of the most important things to keep in mind is that generally 10% or more of your guest list RSVPs "no" and even a higher percentage will turn down your invitation if many of your family and friends live out of town. I know you are all saying to yourself right now as you read this, every person I invite will come to my wedding, but the truth is, they won't...I'm not kidding about the 10%. Also, please don't forget to include yourself and your groom in your count!

BOOKING THE CEREMONY SITE AND RECEPTION VENUE

Booking the ceremony site and reception venue consists of finding availability to secure both locations on your desired date. Some couples choose to have a traditional ceremony in their place of worship followed by a reception in a different location and others will opt for a ceremony and reception at the same venue. Couples who choose a place of worship enjoy upholding religious traditions while couples who decide on one venue for the ceremony and reception have the built-in convenience of a reduced need for additional transportation (money saved!). But don't forget, you'll need a ride home or to the hotel and you'll need space to transport gifts.

If you plan to have your ceremony at a place of worship I recommend asking the following questions:

1. What is the cost to host the ceremony (recommended donation or actual cost)?

2. Will there be a coordinator on site?

3. Will music be included (an organist and vocalist, for example)?

4. What times and days are available for weddings?

5. Are there potential unforeseen conflicts that might impact the time of my wedding?

6. What is included in terms of decor?

If you plan to have your ceremony at the same venue as your reception I recommend asking the following questions:

1. Will the ceremony take place in the same room as the reception?

2. If so, where will cocktail hour take place as the room is changed over from ceremony to reception?

3. Is there an additional cost to host a ceremony?

4. What is included? Chairs? Risers or stage?

5. Is there a sound system to hook up an iPad?

6. Are microphones included?

7. Will any discounts apply if we choose to have the ceremony and reception in the same location?

Budget friendly tip - If you are planning to have your ceremony and your reception at the same location, you will need someone to marry you. I'm aging myself here, however, in the Friends episode where Monica and Chandler got married, Joey actually married them. . . meaning; anyone can go online and get ordained. This is the perfect way to get that one person involved that you didn't know what else to do with! Typically, when a friend is the ordained person who marries you the individual does not charge the couple (money saved!).

RECEPTION VENUE

When choosing a reception venue begin by deciding if you will have a unique site setting or a traditional. This will determine your course of action for booking your venue. This section will help you sort through best options so you can think about what kind of venue meets your needs.

A Traditional Atmosphere - If you choose a traditional atmosphere, begin by researching if wedding packages are offered, and if they are, create a spreadsheet to compare what is included per person at each location. This will vary depending on the type of venue you choose. Most hotels, banquet halls, and country clubs will offer a limited open bar, meal, champagne toast, wine at dinner, linens, and a cake. *Do not* be afraid to negotiate. Venues need your business as much as you need them.

The space you choose will most likely have a minimum revenue requirement. This is the amount of money that you are required to spend in food and beverage before tax and gratuity. Now, if you have close to the amount of people that the room holds, you might meet this minimum revenue in your meals alone. If it does not, then see what else can be added. *Negotiate.*

Let's say your venue requires a $10,000 food & beverage (F&B) minimum. If you have 100 guests with $100 per person for the meal and bar (100 x 100 = $10,000) you will hit the F&B minimum. If 10 of your 100 guests do not show up (remember to account for about 10% of no-shows) you will be $1,000 short of your required minimum (90 x $100 - $9,000) which gives you $1,000 to play with. You can request an additional hour of the bar, a sweet table, or a late night buffet that serves mini cheeseburgers. Who doesn't want a little grease at the end of an open bar?

(These examples are fictitious and do not reflect actual pricing at a specific venue).

How to Negotiate - Negotiation skills are a plus when it comes to planning your wedding but not everyone knows how to successfully apply these skills. Let's learn the basics of negotiation skills with my favorite example - the champagne toast. Suppose your package offers a champagne toast and you don't care for champagne. Determine the monetary value of the toast and try to have it removed from your cost. You can also request to have the monetary amount applied to something else like an additional appetizer. The monetary value might only be about $1.50 or so per guest but that can become an additional piece per person passed during cocktail hour. In other words, that's $1.50 x your number of guests = money that can be spent elsewhere.

Unique Site Venues - If you want a unique site you must keep in mind that you will pay a rental fee that will not include anything other than the actual space. This means you will need to outsource all of your vendors from the meals, to the linens, to the tables and chairs (hello my glorious wedding planner!). Unique sites can be absolutely beautiful *and* an absolute nightmare to coordinate. To avoid developing problems while planning be sure to remain highly organized during the planning process and be sure to appoint a point person who will be in charge of managing all of your vendors during the reception (think Day of Coordinator here).

Questions to ask a venue before booking

When visiting your potential ceremony/reception site, here are some questions you should ask. While it's good to be prepared, don't go in like you know it all simply because you've read this book. Wait until after you've had a tour and listened to their memorized spiel. They will most likely answer a majority of these questions.

1. Is your date available?
2. What is the minimum revenue for the space? Guarantee amount of people?
3. How many people does the room hold?
4. How many weddings take place in one night?
5. What is the cost for exclusive use?
6. Do you have an on-site wedding coordinator? If so, what will she/he set up? How long will she/he stay at the reception?
7. What is the typical time of the reception?
8. Are linens included?
9. Any décor? Centerpieces? Menu Cards?
10. How many servers will you have for my amount of people?
11. How many bartenders?
12. Can we see a sample contract?
13. Is there a private bridal suite?
14. How many bathrooms will be accessible?
15. How many cars does the parking lot hold?
16. Is valet service offered? Is that an additional cost?
17. Is a dance floor included? Is there an additional cost?
18. Will I receive a floor plan?

19. Do you have a safe or designated locked space for wedding gifts?
20. What size/shape tables are included?
21. What time do guests have to be out of the venue? Will we be charged extra if we stay past that time?
22. Can I set up the night before and pick things up (any additional decorations you bring in) the next morning?
23. Does the venue work with any hotels for guests? Is there discounted pricing for guests?
24. Do the bride and groom receive a complimentary room?
25. Is there complimentary shuttle service to and from the hotel to reception site? If not, what is the cost?

PACKAGES

1. How flexible are your packages?
2. Will my prices be locked in if they go up by the time of the wedding?
3. Is there a complimentary food tasting? What is included? How many people can attend?
4. Are coffee and tea included?
5. Is wine included with dinner? What kind? Are there upgrade options? What is the cost?
6. Do you offer kids meals?
7. Do you offer vendor meals?
8. If I were to bring in my own wine do I have to pay a corkage fee?
9. Is there a complimentary champagne toast?

10.   Can you accommodate special dietary requirements?
11.   How long is the open bar? What is the cost to extend?
12.   Who is included in the gratuity?
13.   Is the cake included? If so, what are additional upgrades? Is there a cake tasting?
14.   Is there a fee to cut the cake?

PAYMENTS

1.   What is the required deposit?
2.   Is there a payment schedule? When is the final payment due?
3.   What is the cancellation policy?
4.   Do you offer off peak pricing in certain months? Discounted prices for a Friday, Sunday, or daytime reception?

Friendly Reception Budget Tips

Discounted Meals - Most venue sites will offer vendor meals. This is a less expensive meal to serve to your vendors. It can range from a pasta dish to a deli sandwich with chips, or even the meal you are serving minus the cost of the open bar. There are options, so don't forget to include vendors in your final count. You want to definitely have a meal for your photographer(s) and videographer (if you have one). They are with you the entire day, so if you haven't eaten all day, neither have they.

Another vendor you might want to provide a meal for is the DJ/ Band, but I would ask them if they want one. Some will decline or just take a meal at the DJ table. But please remember to have a seat for them. Include an additional table in your seating chart as the vendor table, even if it's only four people. Keep in mind, your priest or minister should be invited as a guest, not given a vendor meal.

Buffet - Many people think that choosing a buffet over a seated meal is more cost efficient. It usually is not. Everything will be included that the wedding package offers, but the kitchen is not making any less food. In fact, they are usually making more. So the cost is generally not lowered. If you are planning on going this route, be sure the banquet manager or wedding planner is scheduling when guests can move to the buffet line (typically assigned by table). It can become a huge cluster fuck when everyone is rushing to the buffet. I also suggest a double-sided buffet to keep the line moving and multiple buffet set ups or stations depending on your amount of guests.

Kid's Meals - Most venues will offer chicken fingers or a kid friendly meal for guests 12 and under. Guests ages 12-20 a regular meal minus the bar.

Bar - If you are planning on a cash bar at your reception, it is important to give your guests a heads up. I do not recommend this option, but if the cost of a full open bar or a modified bar option (beer, wine and soda) is not within your budget then it's only polite to let your guests know prior to arrival.

There are different tiers of bar packages available so read through your contract to learn about what is included at each tier. You know your guests who will attend your reception. Are they big beer drinkers? Wine drinkers? You can only think of two people who'll order top shelf vodka? A lot of times a modified bar package or middle tier bar package will appeal to all of your guests and not break the bank.

Running a tab can also be another option but I recommend this only if you know for sure very few people will drink or you are having a daytime reception. You don't want a surprise $15,000 bar tab at the end of the night.

Chairs and Linens - I know brides have a certain idea of what they want the room to look like when they walk in for the first time, and are often tempted to splurge on colored chair covers. However, chair covers are usually a costly expense. Chivari chairs are even more expensive and even more uncomfortable. Most reception sites have chairs that blend in with the room. If the chairs provided aren't too offensive I would ditch the cover and spend your money on a million other things. Also see what else the venue has to offer. They might have multiple options included in the price and possibly great vendor rates for specialty linens, if that's a priority for you. The pricing might be cheaper than going straight to the vendor.

CHOOSE YOUR BRIDAL PARTY

Ok, ladies, this is the fun part!

Who should be in the wedding? My advice is to think long and hard about whom is included in your bridal party. While many will feel it is an honor to be part of the big day, asking your nearest and dearest friends and family members will make the experience far more memorable. Also, take into consideration that there is no obligation to include someone in your bridal party that you really don't want to be involved in your wedding.

However, let's look at it for a second from a bridesmaid's perspective. And let's also try to remember when you might have been the bridesmaid and not the bride and thought how annoying some of the bride's requests were to you. This should not change now that the ring is on the other finger.

As we get a little older, chances are, your bridesmaids have been down this road before and unfortunately, you can't help but do the math. Let's list all of the fun events most likely to take place:

1. The first celebration kicking off this year or more of obligations is of course the engagement party. Just a small gathering of your closest friends and family to celebrate your engagement where everyone feels obligated to bring a gift. "You shouldn't have," my ass.

2. The shower. Sometimes multiple showers are planned depending on family dynamic. Please do not expect your bridesmaids to bring a gift for each shower that is thrown. That is just selfish. They might not even be able to go to every single shower.

3. We then have the intimate personal shower, (not a huge expense just a piece of overpriced, raunchy lingerie, guaranteed to never be worn). Of course, this will take place right before the bachelorette party to end all bachelorette parties!

Please keep in mind the expenses listed above are all incurred *before* the actual wedding!

Then we have the obvious expenses.
- The dress. For God's sake spare me the "you can totally wear it again" speech. We all know you can't and won't - unless you buy it off the rack from a well-known store or let them pick their own.

- Shoes. Why would you make your girls spend an obscene amount of money on something no one will see and or pay attention to? If I can't afford a pair of Loubitans for myself, I sure as hell am not getting them for your wedding.

- Hair. Do not make your bridesmaids get their hair done if they don't want to; they can do it themselves instead of getting some terrible up-do. Why wouldn't you want your bridal party to look like themselves?

- Make-up. This one is a must for some people. Professionally done make-up looks so much better in pictures. Besides, have you ever tried to glue on your own fake eyelashes? Not easy my friend, not easy. God, I love fake eyelashes!

- Manis/pedis. Oh, I almost forgot the mini spa excursion of manicures and pedicures that must be scheduled at the most expensive salon in town the day before the BIG DAY. Consider finding a salon that will provide a group rate for you and your bridal party.

- And lastly the wedding gift, which, again, you always feel compelled to give or spend a little more because you are in the wedding.

IT'S EXPENSIVE!

So brides, take a little pressure off your friends, family, and yourself! Do not get mad at your bridal party because you have silly expectations.

Do not have a weekly agenda of "fun" wedding activities for you and your girls for an entire year! The second you make it a rule is the second you take the fun out of it.

Realize they are going to do as much for you as they can but they will most likely not concern themselves with every single detail of your wedding.

I have learned that the fewer amount of people involved, the better the experience actually is! Too many opinions cause confusion, anger, hurt feelings, and anxiety. Try to remember, this is a time to truly enjoy family and friends, not a time to single out the ones who are not doing as much for you as others. Because, honestly, who cares!? This is *your* time! It doesn't mean they like you any less nor are bad friends. Besides, you shouldn't let anyone dictate or determine how great of an experience you will have during this time that should really be between you and your fiancé.

Trust me, your friends really *will* want to take an active role in helping if you remember to be relaxed, laid back, and just have fun! That's what this is all about anyway, right? But then again, there are some friends who are just jealous bitches but somehow finagle their way into your bridal party. Feel free to make them do whatever you want. Ha! Just kidding (are they really friends though?).

Your MOH and BM are responsible for a few things. Here is a list that each person will hopefully take care of.

Responsibilities of the BM

1. Plan the bachelor party.
2. Help groom get dressed.
3. Make sure the groom is sober before taking the plunge.
4. Hold on to the rings until needed.
5. Take care of passing out payments or tips to vendors.
6. Sign the marriage license as official witness.
7. Give a speech/toast
8. Drive the couple to the reception if there is no transportation.
9. Help organize the groomsmen for photos, lineups, and other group responsibilities that day.

Responsibilities of the MOH

1. Plan the bachelorette party.
2. Plan the shower.
3. Be the bride's right-hand woman: dress shop, write out place cards, stuff invitations and help with small details.
4. Help the bride get dressed.
5. Straighten her dress once she reaches the end of the aisle.
6. Hold the bride's flowers during the ceremony.
7. Organize the bridesmaids for photos, lineups, other group responsibilities that day.
8. Bustle the bride's dress before the reception
9. Make a speech/toast

ENGAGEMENT PARTY

This is completely optional and not all couples have an engagement party, but if you are planning one, you'll want to plan it about a year out from the wedding. Your upcoming nuptials are worth celebrating this exciting time! If you're attending one soon for someone else, now is a good time to purchase this book as a gift to them.

CHAPTER CHECKLIST:

_____ Vision the type of wedding you want

_____ Create a budget

_____ Hire a full-time wedding planner

_____ Choose date and time

_____ Create a guest list

_____ Choose a ceremony and reception site

_____ Choose your wedding (bridal) party

_____ Host engagement party

Now Breathe!

STOP AND BREATHE.

Nine times out of 10, when I see couples at our final meeting the week of the wedding they are so beyond done with planning that they just want to go on their honeymoon. How sad is that? After all the work, money, planning, stressing, fighting, blood, sweat, and tears (too dramatic? Perhaps. But maybe not.) you've poured into the "most important day of your life," you'd rather skip it and just get to the honeymoon? NO! It doesn't have to be that way. So, don't let it. I mean, how many times are you going to plan a wedding? Once? Maybe twice? *Enjoy it!*

Just sit back and enjoy your engagement for a little while. Celebrate it. You don't have to have every single detail planned in the first month! In fact, I find that the sooner my clients have their weddings planned and the more time they have to think about things, the bigger a disaster it becomes. They start to overthink, question everything, change color schemes, spend more money on pointless items that are not necessary (who doesn't need a cute little napkin ring around a napkin that's being folded in the wine glass?) because they're bored and or feel like they should be doing something for the wedding even though it's already planned. It's a slippery slope, friends. Don't go there.

CHAPTER 3

Music, Flowers and Photos *Oh My!*

8-10 Months Out

Now that you have had time to enjoy your engagement and have selected your venue, it is time to start booking vendors. Around the 8-10 month mark is when you want to secure your reception entertainment, florist, and photographer.

ENTERTAINMENT

You will want to book your entertainment for your reception. Typically, people will have either a band or DJ. The choice between the two is a personal one you can make with your fiancé. Both a band and a DJ can provide enjoyable entertainment for you and your guests.

DJ

DJs play a major role in a reception. When speaking to a DJ, ask if you can see them in action. You will quickly know their style and if they will be a good fit for you. If you go with a company, they will have different priced DJs depending on experience. Your DJ is also your emcee; so, you want to make sure they know how to run the show.

DJs are the ones making the announcements and sticking to a timeline when it comes to toasts, first dances, and cake cutting. Be sure you like them and that they know what they are doing. Some DJs can set-up perimeter lighting, known as "uplights." Uplights are lights that are cast upwards to create a romantic setting. This lighting comes in a variety of colors. Many DJs will also provide a photo booth, or they can at least recommend a vendor with whom they often work.

Questions to ask a DJ:

1.   How long have you been a wedding DJ?
2.   Will you have an assistant at the wedding?
3.   What happens if you're sick?
4.   Can we come watch you DJ a portion of an actual wedding, with the bride and groom's consent, of course, and see your setup before a wedding starts?
5.   Have you ever emceed at (insert your wedding venue here)?
6.   What do you wear to a wedding?
7.   Do you perform wedding ceremonies?
8.   Do we get to pick the songs for the reception or do you have a set list?
9.   How do you encourage guests to get on the dance floor?
10.   What happens if your equipment malfunctions?
11.   Do you take requests from guests?
12.   Are there additional costs not covered in the contract?
13.   Do you also provide lighting?

14. Do you have a photo booth?
    What's included (props, photos for each
    guest to take home, etc.)?
15. Do you have insurance?
16. Do you require a meal at the reception?
17. Can we see a sample contract?
18. What is the cancellation policy?

You may prefer to have a band over a DJ. Who doesn't love live music? If the right band is chosen, they can be super fun and will definitely get the crowd involved. Something tells me if the main instrument showcased is the accordion, you might be going in the wrong direction. It is rare to have a band member serve as the emcee; so, remember to assign someone to this task. An emcee keeps the flow of the evening and stays on a timeline. If you are having an onsite ceremony, you may be able to get one of the musicians to play live while walking down the aisle, which is a definite positive!

Questions to ask a Wedding Band:

1. How much time is required for setup?
2. What are the load-in requirements? Does the
   band have specific load-in needs?
3. What does the band wear?
4. Can we come and see you perform?
5. What genres do you play?
6. Will the band learn songs that we want
   played?
7. Do you play requests?
8. How much equipment will be used and how
   many musicians will be performing?
9. Can we see a sample contract?

10. Do you require a meal at the reception?
11. Do you have insurance?
12. What size staging space do you require and how many chairs?
13. What is your cancellation policy?

Budget friendly tip - If you are having a more casual wedding and have a fairly tight budget, a great alternative to a DJ or a band is an iPod! Seriously. . . it's all the music you love! Just remember to appoint someone to make announcements and keep the flow of the reception going.

FLORIST

Choosing a florist can be fun because who doesn't love flowers? Your florist will provide not only your personal flowers (your bouquet, bridesmaids' bouquets, boutonnieres, and corsages), but also your ceremony flowers, reception centerpieces, and any additional pieces you prefer, such as cake flowers and a place-card table piece.

Questions to ask a Florist:

1. Can you work within my budget?
2. What flowers are in season at the time of my wedding?
3. How long have you been a wedding florist?
4. Have you worked at my venue and ceremony site?
5. Do you have a portfolio of past weddings I can view?
6. Will you provide me with a sample bouquet and centerpiece?
7. How many weddings do you have in a day?

8.   Do you have payment options? Flat fees?
       Price per item?
9.   Is there an additional delivery charge?
10.   Will you provide a toss bouquet?
11.   Do you provide a ceremony aisle runner?
12.   Do you coordinate the overall look: linens,
       lighting, and table settings as well?
12.   Do you have liability insurance?
13.   Can guests take the centerpieces at the end of
       the evening?
14.   Are the vases rented?
15.   If vases are rented, will you coordinate with
       the venue for pick-up at the end of the
       reception?
16.   Can I see a sample contract?
17.   What is your cancellation policy?

Budget friendly tip - Some venues will provide some sort of centerpiece. Use that as a base to build on if it isn't exactly what you had in mind. This especially comes in handy if the centerpiece included offers fresh flowers from a florist!

If nothing is included, choose a glass votive, from a craft store and add votive candles and rose petals (grocery stores have great flowers) for a romantic, cost-efficient setting. Or head to the local farmers market and pick out colorful fruit, submerge them in water in a cylinder vase, and set a candle on top. This is a vibrant, sophisticated, and inexpensive alternative to flowers.

You can also "reuse" flowers. For example, you can bring your ceremony flowers into your reception to be used as part of your centerpiece or any additional way you choose. Also, line-up small vases along the edge of your head table and place your bouquets and your bridesmaids' bouquets in them to create a beautiful look. That was easy!

PHOTOGRAPHER

Capturing memories will help you remember the visuals of your special day. So, choose your photographer wisely. Much like DJs and florists, photographers will offer different price options. Seek out recommendations from friends and family who have used photographers at their weddings. Look at the photographer's actual work in the studio, not just on his or her website. This is one area I would try not to skimp on. These photos will be with you for the rest of your life. You definitely want experience, professionalism, and reputation from your photographer.

*Questions to ask a Photographer

1. What is your primary style? Photojournalistic? Traditional?
2. How many photographers will be with you? What is the additional cost?
3. What happens if you are ill?
4. How many weddings have you photographed?
5. Will you color-correct my images?
6. What kind of packages do you offer?
7. How long will it take to get our proofs and albums?
8. What digital options are available post event?

9.   What attire will you wear during the wedding and reception?
10.   Can we see a sample album?
11.   Can we see a sample contract?
12.   Do you have insurance?
13.   What is your cancellation policy?

**Similar questions are applicable to videographers as well

Budget friendly tip - Look for a company that does both photography and videography. Book 'em both and cut a deal!

SHOP FOR YOUR DRESSES!!!

You might want to start by researching different types of gowns on the Internet and cut out pictures from bridal magazines. Have some ideas in mind so you are not completely overwhelmed when you walk into your first bridal shop. And let's be real, it's hard enough to find a cute shirt for date night let alone your wedding dress!

Do the same for bridesmaids' dresses. Have an idea of color and a style that will work for *all* of your bridesmaids. Are they 6-foot-tall supermodels? Are half your girls pregnant? Do you even want everyone in the same dress? Be considerate and remember what looks good on you might not be the right fit for them; so, bring them along for the fun!

Register

Gift registry might be one of the most exciting moments of wedding planning! You and your fiancé literally walk into a store and create this magical wish list of items that other people will buy for you! That sure to never-be-used waffle maker you've always dreamed of can finally be yours! Awesome!

Additional Insurance

Most vendors and venues will have insurance. If they can't provide insurance, think twice about hiring them. The last thing you need to worry about is DJ Shadey McShaderson breaking something at your venue.

Contract any Rental Items

Rental companies are vital when planning a wedding at a unique venue. You will want to start reaching out to rental companies if you choose a location that does not include tables, chairs, silverware, and other necessities. You can typically find one rental company that will provide all of these items. Below are some helpful tips when ordering these items on your own.

Tables and Linens

Tables you will need for your reception include the following:

Head table - A traditional head table includes rectangle tables pushed together to accommodate the number of people in the bridal party. If you have a large number, you might want to consider having a double-tiered head table, where one table is on risers behind the other. The bride and groom are seated on the top riser. The order of the processional is the order in which the wedding party is seated. For instance, the MOH and the BM are seated beside the bride and groom.

Place-card Table - Usually a rectangle table is used, but I have used a round place-card table as well. It is NOT easy arranging place-cards in a circle, but it looks kind of cool.

Cake Table - Depending on the size of your cake, a 60"-round table is frequently used. I see no reason for a 72" round to be used either...well, unless you have a seriously oversized cake. Spread candles and simple rose petals around the base of the cake for an elegant and romantic look.

DJ Table - The DJ will most likely only need a rectangle table as well, but check to make sure.

The tables listed above will require skirting. Skirting is the draping of a table to make it look more formal and elegant.

Guests Tables - I'm pretty sure we don't need a definition here . . . but just in case, they are the tables where your guests sit.

Table sizes

Figure out what size tables the venue has or you will need to supply. If you are going with round or square tables, 60" **will comfortably hold 6-10 guests** each, while, **72" will comfortably hold 8-12 people.**

If they offer both sizes, this definitely gives you some flexibility with the seating chart. You most likely will not get a perfect 8 or 10 at each.

If you are choosing **rectangle tables (also known as dining room style), they are typically 6' by 30" and can fit 6-8** people depending on if you're using the head of each table.

Leave about 60" between each table. Don't forget that! You will have a lot of people moving around. Make sure the staff has enough room to properly serve each guest and that your guests have enough room to pull out their chairs.

Linens

If your venue does not provide you with linens, here is a quick guide to linens for popular table sizes. These dimensions are based on floor-length linens, which will hide unsightly table legs.

For **60" round tables** you will want a **120" tablecloth**. If you are choosing to add an overlay, you will want this to be **90."** An overlay is an additional linen piece that lies over the tablecloth, covering the top of the table and slightly around the sides. Overlays add a pop of color or shimmer to your tables. Skirting for the cake table will require **16."**

With a **72" round table,** use a **132"** tablecloth, **90"** overlay, and **19"** skirting. A **6' by 30" rectangle tables** will need a **90" x 132" floor-length tablecloth.**

Remember to add **17' skirting** for the head table, place-card table, and DJ table.

Bartenders and Wait staff

Usually you will have one bartender per every 100 guests and usually every person complains about this. You can, of course, pay for an additional bartender if you feel this wouldn't work for your party because your guests are big drinkers (which we hear often). Most bartenders can handle this, and depending on the actual size of the bar, there won't be enough room for three. If you fear long lines at the bar and don't want to pay for an additional bartender, an option is to have two members of the wait staff greet your guests as they come into the room with trays of white and red wine as well as champagne. This will help eliminate long lines.

You should have one server for every 2-3 tables. This is something the banquet manager or banquet captain will handle, but be sure you have enough staff. What's the difference between a manager and a captain? I'm happy you asked. If you are having your wedding at a venue that has multiple weddings or events taking place, the banquet manager will oversee all the events, while the banquet captain is in charge of your room only.

Food

Now is a good time to start thinking about the kind of food you'd like to serve your guests. I would start with what might realistically fit within your budget. While everyone would love the surf and turf, sometimes the chicken piccata works just as well. It's also important to remember that there's no way your pre-selected meal is going to possibly please everyone. And guess what, it's ok. I would, however, choose a meal that a majority of your guests would enjoy. For example, if you are a vegan, I would not suggest serving a four course vegan meal to 175 people.

Out-of-Town Arrangements

If you can believe this, in the olden days, the bride's family would actually pay for all the accommodations for out-of-town guests, including airfare! *Wtf!* Since this is probably not an option these days, nor should it be, you want to start blocking rooms at the hotel of your choice. Keep in mind the budget of your out-of-town guests.

CHAPTER CHECKLIST:

_____ Book your entertainment

_____ Book your florist

_____ Book your photographer

_____ Start dress shopping

_____ Register

_____ Examine the need for additional insurance

_____ Contract rental items needed

_____ Start thinking about the kind of food
you want at your wedding

_____ Reserve accommodations (block rooms)
for out-of-town guests

Chapter 4

Sunset beaches with Costumed Characters. . . *wait* what?

4-8 Months out

THEMES

Themes can be an easy way to stay focused and organized when planning your wedding. They can be really different, creative, and a fun way to make it your own, if done properly. When choosing the right theme for you, I suggest something that has a shared meaning between you and your fiancé. Not a childhood obsession that you can't seem to shake. Who doesn't love famous cartoon characters? Most of my childhood revolved around New Kids on the Block, but unless Joey Mac is literally singing "Please Don't Go Girl" to me at the reception, in which case, the wedding itself might be in question, I will refrain from having life-size cutouts of my personal fab 5 as "guests."

In other words, themes can also go terribly wrong. Let's try to remember, we're all adults. It might be time to hang up the idea of your favorite amusement park theme, or a princess fairy tale theme, or a favorite ceramic figurine theme. Now don't get me wrong, I was a diehard collector of Precious Moments®.

For birthdays, Christmas, or any occasion I would receive a gift, my request was the latest figurine to hit the market. After all, they too, made their First Holy Communion! But, then one day, I had a long talk with myself and decided it was time to stop, time to give it all up, yet cherish the memories I had . . . I was 13.

Every single couple tells me they want their wedding to be unique. Of course, what makes your wedding unique is that it's your wedding. However, if you are planning a traditional church ceremony and reception, chances are I've seen it before. It is rare that I am actually invited to an experience . . . a time warp . . . a different country or city . . . that truly makes a wedding different.

There are some really great theme ideas out there. Do your research and really make it authentic. Start with a color scheme to go with your theme. This will speak volumes.

Below are a few of my favorite ideas to get your creative juices flowing!

Vintage - Well, because who doesn't love past eras? Try for a glitzy 1920's theme. A great way to incorporate this is to have worn birdcages included in your wedding decorations to create a retro look. Think pomander style flowers, have your bridesmaids dress in fun, yet elegant flapper-style dresses, and choose simple jewelry. Pearls and a feathered headband will fit this era perfectly. Use vintage postcards as part of your invitation, menu card, or centerpieces. These are great ways to feel the vibe of the era.

A 1960s *Mad Men* Theme - This is my ultimate favorite as I believe I was born in the wrong era. Guys, think skinny ties, fedora hats, and typewriter cuff links. Ladies, let's go with tea- length dresses and pinned-up hair, and full-length gloves. Brides can bring white opera gloves back into fashion! Decorate with vintage suitcases and typewriters. Offer your signature drink as a martini or Manhattan. Serve mini cake shots for dessert!

Hollywood Glam - Think elegant and ritzy—not the tabloid trash of current day. The main colors should be black and white with very simple pops of red, pink, or gold. Create a red carpet for guests. The photographer can take each couple's picture as they arrive. Not only does this add to the theme, but ensures you have a photo of every one of your guests. Centerpieces should include black vases with red roses. Add black feathers and beaded stems for a glamorous look. Font on invitation and menu cards should be elegant. Bring in movie clap boards that have your names and wedding date written on them. And, of course, adorn the wedding and reception with lots of candlelight. For the highest level of keeping with this theme, request a black-tie reception.

Rustic/Barn/Shabby Chic - Ladies and gents, break out those cowboy boots! Have the setting in a rustic barn which is absolutely gorgeous when decorated. An outdoor tent works well too (I don't mean a tent you'd pitch in your backyard. Think of a beautiful white weatherproof event tent from a reputable rental company. This will eliminate the need for a Plan B). Ladies, opt for short bridesmaid dresses and fellas think a little more casual with vests as opposed to a full-on suit. Décor should include lots of lanterns, barrels, and candle lights. You might also want to incorporate hay and wheat strands, which surprisingly can be beautiful when mixed together! Centerpieces can go in mason jars or milk jugs. Old window panes add a perfect touch for your seating chart. As a cute wedding favor, give mini mason jars filled with all the fixings for s'mores. Burlap makes an ideal table runner. If you're handwriting signs to display on the sweet table, try using pieces of wood or chalk boards. This style of wedding can be tremendously fun with easy do-it-yourself projects.

Boho/Bohemian/Hippy - If this is your type of theme outdoors is the only way to go. This is for the bride who is laid-back, free-spirited, and completely unconventional. (What a breath of fresh air!) Think flowing dresses, florals, lace, ruffles, floral headbands, and open seating for your guests. Natural sunlight and nature are the ideal backdrops for your reception. Perhaps walk down the aisle to a simple guitar strum.

Travel Themes - If you've traveled to a specific country together or have a mutual favorite city, make the destination your theme! You can even bring the theme of your dream honeymoon into your reception. Whatever you choose you can create fun passport cards with your names and wedding date printed on them. Luggage tags are befitting wedding favors. Incorporate the cuisine from your favorite country. Your wedding menu will surely be more interesting than the usual dishes so often served. Bring in subtle hints of the country's signature flower and colors. Play authentic music of your favorite destination to enhance the cultural theme.

Italy - Create a quaint Italian village in any venue. Use big umbrellas over large dining-room style seating with centerpieces of tree branches with flowers entwined. Bring as much of the outdoors in. A lot of candlelight adds to the romantic setting. Mini Italian wine bottles will make the perfect favor. Serve small portions of spaghetti and meatballs as part of your hors d'oeuvres hour.

Paris - The Eiffel tower can be used for multiple purposes: on invitations, menu cards, place-card holders, favors, a design on your wedding cake, or a cake topper. Do not put it on everything as you want an ambiance of elegance. Choose a light pink as your wedding color and include pink roses. Serve French pastries as part of your dessert or on the sweet table.

United States - Whether you prefer the East Coast, the West Coast, the Midwest, or the South there are a ton of ways you can carry such themes into your wedding plans.

> **East Coast.** Think nautical, lighthouses, and seafood. Consider lobster rolls for appetizers and crab cakes as part of your meal. Choose navy blue as your main color.

> **West Coast** - Use bright colors like coral and seafoam and serve an avocado with water for dinner . . . kidding... but you can see where I'm going here.

> **Midwest** - Well that's easy, I'm from Chicago...meat with a side a meat wrapped in bacon. Throw in a pizza or beef sandwich and fries and serve mini hot dogs at the end of the evening. Hold the ketchup, please.

> **The South -** Think comfort food like fun mac-and-cheese balls or a fried chicken and waffle skewer as an appetizer. The South is known for pies; make it your dessert or favor.

While incorporating your favorite things to draw upon a theme as a couple is great, but remember to keep it simple and classy, not cheesy. If you absolutely can't let go of the idea of costumed characters, perhaps just have their logo on the corner of your dinner menu or designed on your wedding cake or invitation. Do not have the actual characters plastered on every single part of your décor. Or better yet, save such themes for your kid's 1st birthday party.

One last thought, if a theme is chosen, don't do it half-assed. Start with your invitation to build excitement for your big day! Continue to carry this through to every last detail, from the food to the favors to the music and decoration. Give your guests a memorable experience they will be talking about for years to come. This will undoubtedly make your wedding unique.

~Personal Story~

The Bridal Blues

Oh man. I will *never* forget this gal. I had a bride who stated, "I love blue" during our first meeting when I asked about thoughts on theme and color scheme. *Ok,* I thought, *what the hell does that mean?* Well, let me tell you, this bride wanted to make *everything* blue. She wanted crystal blue chairs, blue candle holders with blue candles accompanied by blue crystals hanging from curly willow, and blue sequin floor-length table linens (Do those even exist? If so, they shouldn't!). Oh, it doesn't stop there. She envisioned blue rhinestone framed wedding invitations, menu cards, table numbers, and place cards painted with clear blue glitter. I seriously wanted to ask her if she shit blue! No joke. So, after hearing all of her blue-*tiful* ideas I knew we had to reel this in before we called the local kindergarten class to help decorate her wedding reception.

I'm all for a little blue or a monochromatic color scheme, but yikes. It took a while, but after a few meetings we scaled down the blue and decided on a champagne color scheme with blue highlights. Tasteful blue rhinestones were placed on the corners of her place cards and menu cards, and the table numbers were in pale, muted blue frames. The table linens were floor-length satin champagne with pale blue table runners. The tables were adorned with votive candles, blue and clear scattered crystals, and short round floral arrangements with white and champagne florals in a clear, blue bowl vase. She got her blue, but in a much more tasteful way.

When coming up with a color scheme or theme for your wedding less can actually be more. Don't drown your guests in your inspiration, instead highlight it. Whether it is a costumed character from an amusement park, the color blue, or even bling, always remember, and I cannot emphasize this enough, keep it classy.

PLAN YOUR HONEYMOON

Now is the time to order or update your passports and book your honeymoon. Research places you've always wanted to visit and be sure you are not going in the height of hurricane, monsoon, or any other storm season. Talk to your friends. Where did they honeymoon or vacation? Think about if you want a facility-only resort or an all-inclusive (the answer is almost always "yes please!" for an all-inclusive resort).

Consider using a travel agent because consultations tend to be complimentary. Use your network and online resources when you take time to plan your perfect honeymoon. You never want to wing it, especially in a foreign country. Be smart and play safe.

SAVE THE DATE

Decide if save-the-dates are even necessary for your wedding. I definitely recommend save the dates if you are having a destination wedding or a holiday wedding, or even a shotgun wedding. This is your wedding, not a housewarming or BBQ; so, a social media group message does not count as a save-the-date.

ORDER INVITATIONS

With the billions of font type available on most computers, invitations are something you can easily design yourself! You can also design the place cards, thank you cards, and shower invitations. This will save you hundreds of dollars, but it may make you a little crazy. There are *a lot* of choices! This is also a great time to utilize your computer savvy cousin in college who'd be happy to help for payment in pizza and beer. We all know someone or know someone who knows someone who's amazing with computers; now's the time to call in that favor. If you decide to order invitations through a company you can select online companies or traditional brick and mortar print shops.

FAVORS

Think long and hard about this one. What does one single person actually do with a 3x5 picture frame that their place-card comes in? Aside from throwing it in the garbage, they might "accidentally" leave it on the table at the end of the night. Money wasted. Do everyone a favor and choose something edible (those almost never go to waste), or make a donation to your favorite charity on behalf of yourselves and your guests. It will definitely be money better spent.

Contract ceremony entertainment

Are you getting married on site? Would you like some music playing while you all walk down the aisle? Now is the time to book your ceremony musicians. Often times you can ask the ceremony site if anything is included. For example, if you choose a church, is an organist included? Otherwise, ask for recommendations or preferred vendor list from the church or ceremony site venue.

Formal wear

Ok guys, here is literally the *one* job you have to do. Go find a tuxedo or suit to rent. Wear it. Return it. Done.

Wedding bands

Get them...as proof you *finally* landed someone. Ha! Most likely, your engagement ring already has a matching wedding band or you have the choice to create one. Oh, and guys, you should get one too. And wear it. Have fun with it!

Marriage counseling/pre Cana

Attending classes 4-6 months before the wedding date is typically required for certain religious ceremonies... If you want to be married, attend the class 4-6 months before your wedding. (For example, Pre-Cana course is required for those married in the Catholic church.)

Book your DOC

If you are choosing to have a Day-of-Coordinator as opposed to a full-on wedding planner, book them now. Save your sanity...they're worth every penny.

CHAPTER CHECKLIST:

_____ Plan a theme

_____ Plan your honeymoon

_____ Send save-the-dates

_____ Think about invitations

_____ Consider favors

_____ Contract ceremony entertainment

_____ *Guys* - Choose your formalwear to rent
or purchase

_____ Purchase wedding bands

_____ Register for marriage counseling, if necessary

_____ Hire your DOC- Day-of-Coordinator

Chapter 5

You're Getting Closer!

2-3 Months out

Ok ladies, are we still breathing? Are you all still with me? Now that we've done a majority of the heavy lifting, we can start having a little more fun. Two to three months out is when you want to select a wedding cake, be a guest at your shower and bachelorette party, purchase gifts for your bridal party, and participate in hair and makeup trials. So basically, pamper the shit out of yourself.

WEDDING CAKE

Now is the time to meet with bakeries to plan your wedding cake! I cannot think of a better tasting than the cake tasting. . . ok, maybe a wine tasting. . . no, no, I still choose the cake tasting. You'll definitely want to meet with bakers who specialize in wedding cakes. All bakeries will offer cake tastings where you'll have the option to sample different flavors mixed with different fillings. Learn the difference between buttercream and fondant, and choose your cake design.

If your reception site offers a wedding cake, go with it. This will typically be a buttercream cake. Fondant might look nice, but it tastes awful and most bakers can do amazing designs with buttercream.

Unless you're vying for a spot on the latest wedding reality show (that never talks pricing!), stick with what is included. Trust me. The cake will sit on your dance floor for an hour. You'll get great pictures with it and then slice it into hundreds of pieces. The end.

Budget Friendly Tip - If the venue offers a dessert other than cake as part of the package, know that fake cakes do exist! You can have a faux multi-tiered cake with only the top tier being real for you to cut during the cake-cutting ceremony. Less money. Less waste.

~PERSONAL STORY~

No Cake For You Bride

I have a friend of mine who isn't a big cake person. (I know, I don't know what's wrong with her either.) I negotiated with her venue to provide a variety of mini cupcakes as opposed to a wedding cake. The venue happily agreed to this. She is big on ice cream; so, she and her fiancé ordered a small ice cream cake to cut and take pictures with. I believe they ended up eating and sharing their ice cream wedding cake after the reception too. It was messy yet memorable. Now on their anniversary they always go to that ice cream shop and order a milkshake as a reminder of their wedding cake.

ATTEND YOUR BRIDAL SHOWER

There really isn't one set person who hosts the bridal shower anymore. The host can be a bridesmaid or sister, aunt, mother-of-the-bride, future mother-in-law, or a group of people. Whatever the case may be, the hostess should consult with the bride to create the guest list. Anyone invited to the shower should also be invited to the wedding.

Some brides spend an hour or more opening gifts. Yay spoons! What an interesting salad bowl (said no one ever!). After a while you start losing the crowd's interest. One fun idea is to have guests bring the gifts unwrapped and you can display them on the table for everyone to see. As exciting as your wedding is, no one wants to watch you open presents for four hours. Another great idea is to do a gift card shower. Maybe you and your fiancé are combining homes or you've recently moved in together and have a lot of housewares already. Your shower invitation can list up to 6 places where you'd like gift cards, and then enjoy your guests at your shower instead of spending time opening gifts. Mingle, cocktail, eat, and use those gift cards as you need them. There are also a lot of honeymoon websites where people request their shower guests to donate funds. I mean, who wouldn't want to build an account that goes towards your once in a lifetime trip to some fabulous destination that looks *amazing!* Or . . . you can register for a gravy boat. Do you even have to think about this?

TRANSPORTATION

At this time, you'll want to book your limousine, trolley, Bentley (stop it), or rideshare driver (kidding, or am I?). Remember you'll need several rides: from the place you are getting ready to the ceremony site, and then to the reception site. Also remember to make plans for transportation to wherever you're staying that night. I highly recommend taking that ride to your ceremony with just you and your dad, or whoever is walking you down the aisle. Enjoy that *"holy wow!* I'm getting married can you believe this dad"* moment. This is a big day for him too. Their baby isn't a baby anymore.

MAIL INVITATIONS

Mail your invitations. Don't forget the self-addressed stamped envelope for the RSVP! Find out when your final guest count is required from your caterer or venue. The return date for your RSVPs should be about two weeks before the final guest count is due. This should give you plenty of time to call, email, or text those people who for some reason couldn't get that little card back to you in the last two months. And yes, this does happen…with every single wedding I've planned.

GIFTS

Now is a good time to purchase gifts for your parents, bridal party, and ushers that you will bring to the rehearsal dinner. Brides and grooms often purchase gifts for each other that are given the day of the wedding. The Internet is a great resource for this kind of stuff. You can never go wrong with jewelry or alcohol. If you and your fiancé decide not to exchange gifts, maybe have the BM and MOH present a card or little love note to your soon-to-be spouse. It's the little things after all, right?

HAIR and MAKE-UP TRIALS

Of course, you want to have a practice run for both hair and makeup before game time! A great time to plan this is the day of your shower, bachelorette party, or even for your engagement photos. You don't want to be all dolled-up with nowhere to go! This will also allow you to get opinions from your friends and family regarding your desired look for the big day. Then again, I'm not sure if this is a good or bad thing.

BACHELORETTE PARTY

Really think about the bachelorette party and the age of your party guests. If you want a destination send off, do not make it mandatory for everyone to attend, and definitely do not make them feel bad for choosing not to attend.

Whether it's a relaxing weekend with a few friends at a spa or an epic (believe me, they're never epic) weekend with 25 friends in Las Vegas (which is not a recipe for disaster at all), the choice is up to you. Always consider your guests and be wary of the cost. Not only are they going to have to pay their own way, but they will somehow feel it is expected to foot the bill for you. Please don't let them.

To all those who've been in a bridal party: Why do we do this to ourselves? Why do we feel a sense of guilt into paying for everything when we were asked to stand up in a wedding? Think about how ridiculous that sounds.

If you are a little older maybe combine the bachelor and bachelorette party. BBQs or wine and beer tastings are perfect for a coed atmosphere.

HOTEL WELCOME GIFTS

This doesn't have to be extravagant or mandatory, but putting together a little welcome basket is a nice idea to let your guests know you're happy they're here! Fill bags with sweet and salty snacks to tide them over before dinner or after the celebration. A simple bottle of water, or if you have a bigger budget, miniature bottles of wine, along with a bag of pretzels, a candy bar, and an aspirin packet will be much appreciated at 2am post-wedding. Customize the welcome gift to fit your location. For example, if you're in Chicago, include Chicago's signature mix popcorn.

CHAPTER CHECKLIST:

_____ Wedding Cake

_____ Shower

_____ Transportation

_____ Mail invitations

_____ Gifts

_____ Hair and makeup trial

_____ Bachelorette Party

_____ Hotel welcome gifts

love

Chapter 6

(Cue the music) It's the Final Countdown. . .

30 Days out

We are so close we can almost taste it! But, there are a few more very necessary steps we need to take before getting to the isle. This chapter will ensure you have everything needed in the event of an emergency. Be sure to finalize details so all vendors are on the same page, and don't forget that marriage license!

SURVIVAL KIT

Every bride and bridesmaid should carry around a bridal survival kit. This will be especially helpful if you are not having a wedding planner.

BRIDAL SURVIVAL KIT

_____ Safety Pins

_____ Bobby Pins

_____ Hairspray

_____ Deodorant (spray-on so everyone can use it)

_____ Aspirin and Ibuprofen

_____ Tissue

_____ Water

_____ Rubber bands

_____ Flip flops or a pair of comfortable shoes

_____ Adhesive bandage

_____ Small brush or comb

_____ Tiny sewing kit

_____ Tampons (ugh! Hopefully not for the bride)

_____ Superglue

_____ Laundry-detergent stick

_____ Breath mints

_____ Double-sided fabric tape

_____ A small bag of pretzels or crackers

_____ Wet wipes

_____ Floss pics . . . you should never neglect
your gums

_____ Facial oil dabbers

FINALIZE VENDOR DETAILS

Now is the time to get all of the final details
organized with your vendors. Again, something your
wedding planner or DOC would do, but the following
is good information for you to know as well.

Photographers - If you have specific photographs
you want taken, as the day is fairly chaotic and you
don't want to miss taking a picture with grandma,
provide the photographer with a list to ensure that you
don't forget any important shots. Be realistic when
stopping at post-ceremony photo locations. Of course,
you want to go back to the park you walked through
on your first date or that really cool mural that's next
to this strip mall where you grew up. Are these places
close to your ceremony? Are they on opposite ends of
town? Did you decide to have 27 people in your
bridal party who you now have to transport around
town and group together for these pictures? Your
photographer is not a magician. She cannot teleport
you and your bridal party to four locations, take
numerous photos, and have you back for cocktail
hour in the *one* hour timeslot you allotted for pictures.
If your wedding is in the suburbs, but you *have* to
have city shots, think about taking pictures before the
wedding if timing permits. I think the bad luck theory
of seeing the bride before the wedding has gone out
the window these days.

DJs/Band - You might want to provide a "do" and "do not" playlist. The "do not" playlist is just as important as the "do" playlist. If you don't want to do the chicken dance, they need to know. Although they will usually ask you this, now is the time to finalize. You'll also want to go over all of your special dances: father/daughter, mother/son, the first dance for the bride and groom, that traditional family Polish polka, and whatever else is really important to you. You also need to let them know if they're allowed to take requests. Remember, however, the bride and groom can trump song choice requests at any time. I recommend a "no mic policy," meaning this isn't drunken karaoke time . . . unless that's what you want. Then have at it!

BEO - Your venue is going to present you with your final BEO, which will have all of your details and pricing. Read this *very* carefully! Is your guest count accurate (although usually absolute final count isn't due until about a week before the wedding)? Is the menu correct? Does your floor plan look ok? Did they add that random vodka they said they would because your dad drinks it? If these specific details are not in the BEO, chances are they will not make it into the reception. This is the document everyone (banquet managers, wedding planners, bartenders, and chefs) works from so make sure nothing is forgotten. Check to see that your timeline is accurate and pricing is in line because you don't want to receive a surprise bill the night of. Wait? We ran a tab? It's $5,000? I thought we had a bar package? Whoopsy!

Florist and Rentals - Review your contracts and make sure nothing is missing. Double check load-in and load-out details and make sure this schedule also works with your venue. Check to see if the florist will collect the vases you most likely rented for centerpieces at the end of the evening. If not, make sure you can leave them overnight for your florist to retrieve them the next day. At this time you should also receive your Day of Contact. Make sure you include the contact person's name and phone number in a safe place. Do I hear another spreadsheet being made? Great idea!

FINAL GOWN FITTING

The next time you wear this dress will be on your wedding day! Make sure your final fitting leaves enough time for alterations and the final steaming. Your seamstress does not have a magic wand (I know, no one does and its super annoying!); so, now is not the time to add another layer or reconfigure the bustle. Now is the time when your dress is complete and you check to see if it fits perfectly. Then don't crash diet or live on juice and kale. Just have one donut instead of six and you'll be fine.

MARRIAGE LICENSE

Do you want to be legally married? If so, you need this paper within 30 days of your wedding. Research ahead of time where to get it. And then go get it. And then get married. And then live happily ever after . . . and be recognized by your state as a legally married couple.

FINALIZE RSVPs

Yes, the moment we've all been waiting for: calling your invited guests that took it upon themselves to never respond! It will happen; just prepare yourself to track them down. Rude, I know, but it happens. You'd think all adults can RSVP, some cannot and will not. And then you'll ask your fiancé if his groomsmen are bringing guests and they'll respond with "I think so" or "obviously he's coming, he's in the wedding." Awesome, thanks! So be prepared to contact some of your guests. I'd like to say divide and conquer, but if you want something done . . . you know where I'm going with this, right?

PROGRAMS

Now this might not be something you even need. If you're having a religious ceremony then, yes, put together a program of those participating and the order of events, music, and proceedings. Not everyone attending your ceremony may be familiar with your religious affiliation. If your ceremony is outside, maybe include at least one sheet for your guests to repurpose as a fan. If your ceremony and reception are in the same venue and it's going to be a whole 20 minutes then maybe you don't really need a program. Not every ceremony requires a program, so before you hit print, consider if you really want them.

CHAPTER CHECKLIST

_____ Prepare survival kit

_____ Finalize vendor details

_____ Final gown fitting

_____ Marriage license

_____ Finalize RSVPs

_____ Programs for the ceremony

Chapter 7

SHOWTIME (insert jazz hands)!

WEDDING WEEK

This chapter outlines a schedule for your final week. Finalizing details, such as the order in which the wedding party walks down the aisle to the timeline of the reception, will minimize problems or delays.

Check lists are included so you don't forget any important items for the big day! One of my most favorite things to do in life is to write lists and check things off! It feels so good knowing you accomplished that one little or big task! That's normal, right? Yeah. . . it's totally normal.

CEREMONY CHECKLIST

_____ The RINGS!!!

_____ Marriage License orCertificate

_____ A copy of your vows if you are writing your own.

_____ Programs*

_____ Unity Candle or Sand*

_____ Aisle runner*

_____ Readings and poems. Be sure you have
a printed copy for guests who will be
reading.

_____ Florals including ceremonial, altar, and pew or
row arrangements. Remember to have
boutonnieres and corsages for grandparents,
readers, and musicians.

*These items are optional.

On-site ceremony will also include:

1. An officiant
2. Music. You pay your DJ/Band for an
    additional few hours, hire a separate
    musician (violinist, harpist, or pianist),
    or create a ceremony playlist and
    assign someone to play and pause on
    your MP3 player.
3. Microphones will be needed if you
    want guests to hear you recite your
    vows. The venue might provide lapel
    mics, otherwise your DJ or whoever is
    providing the ceremony music might
    be able to include microphones. A
    standing microphone will be handy if
    you have multiple people reading.
4. Aisle Runner.

If your ceremony and reception are at the same site
take note that the venue will most likely offer chairs
and a riser for the bride and groom and that is it. You
would be responsible for any other décor you choose.

ORDER OF CEREMONY PROCESSIONAL

One of the most exciting parts of a wedding ceremony is the processional. Guests will arrive and wonder which side to sit on. Cue the ushers! Ushers, who can also be groomsmen, seat guests of the bride on the left of the aisle and guests of the groom on the right. Remind ushers to leave the first couple of rows empty for immediate family.

Seating of the Parents - Once the processional music begins honored guests may be seated. The groom's family is seated to the right side of the aisle and the bride's to the left. Remember to have an appointed person to walk grandparents if they are solo and the mother of the bride. This is usually a sibling, cousin, or close family member. Even if they are standing up in the wedding there will be plenty of time for them to get back in line.

1. Seating of the groom's grandparents.

2. Seating of the bride's grandparents

3. Seating of the groom's parents

4. Seating of the bride's mother

Bridal Processional Begins

- Officiant and groom enter, as well as groomsmen if they are not escorting the bridesmaids down the aisle.
- Bridesmaids enter and walk down the aisle one at a time. If groomsmen are escorting bridesmaids, they enter together. Bridesmaids will veer to the left and groomsmen to the right.
- Maid or matron of honor enters. If she is being escorted by the best man, they enter together.
- Flower girl and ring bearer enter. If they are not walking together, the ring bearer enters before the flower girl.

The Wedding March Begins

The Bride and her father enter as soon as the wedding march begins. The bride walks on the left side of her father as the groom stands on the right side of the altar (or wherever your ceremony is taking place) replacing her father as he "gives her away" (*tear).

A personal side note to the grooms out there: my favorite part of the ceremony is to watch your reaction to seeing the bride for the first time. It truly is something special . . . so make it good! I'll be watching.

RECEPTION CHECKLIST

Below is a suggested checklist for your reception. You may not have all of the items, but it is helpful to check things off so you don't forget them! Remember to put your place cards in alphabetical order and not according to table number. When your guests look for their place cards, they have no idea what table they're sitting at; so, arranging the cards alphabetically will eliminate a whole lot of confusion for everyone.

Wedding Reception Checklist:

_____Place Cards (in alphabetical order)

_____Guest Book and Pen

_____Toasting Glasses

_____Cake Knife and Server

_____Favors

_____Menu Cards

_____Cake Topper

_____Money Bag/Box

List any additional items:

If the florist is providing fresh flowers on the cake and a toss bouquet, please make sure you let the venue know to ensure they are delivered.

Who sets up all this crap?

It is also extremely important to know who is in charge of setting up all of these items. For example, if you have an onsite coordinator/ banquet captain, or banquet manager through your venue, he or she will most likely set up your place-card table, your favors, set out your cake knife and server, and toasting glasses. You definitely want to know this information before the big day. If one is not appointed to these tasks and you are not hiring a wedding planner, I highly recommend delegating these tasks in advance. You'll also want to find out the same for the end of the night as well. Will the banquet captain store everything in an office for you to collect the next day? Do you need to take everything with you that night? Who will transport your gifts and cards? These are all important tasks to delegate in advance so you're not scrambling the day of.

Your florist will set up all of your centerpieces and any additional pieces you have.

If you chose additional linens like chivari chairs, chair covers, upgraded table cloths, or overlays, they will be handled by the linen company.

Also keep in mind the order of the set up. Your main contact at your venue (and/or your planner) should coordinate everything, but it is good information to know.

The venue will need to have the floorplan (tables and chairs) in place first. Next, the linen company will come and arrange the linens, chairs, and chair covers. Your florist will then adorn the tables with your centerpiece and floral arrangements. And lastly, the venue will set the tables and add final touches, such as, menu cards, table numbers, and tea lights. Just a little inside scoop about what will occur at the venue before your arrival . . . no thanks needed.

HOTEL CHECKLIST

_____ Overnight bag

_____ Toiletries

_____ Day after outfit

_____ Delegate who will return men's formalwear

_____ Wedding night outfit (Maybe that overpriced piece of raunchy lingerie you received at the bachelorette party will come in handy after all. Or, now that you're married bring those oversized flannel PJs...Let's be real!)

_____ Hotel guest gift bags

_____ Final room block list

_____ Post wedding brunch BEO (if applicable)

_____ Transportation home

_____ Pick-up plan for gifts, cake, and reception items (toasting flutes, cake cutter, picture frames used on place-card table, etc.)

SAMPLE RECEPTION TIMELINE

This is based on a traditional wedding reception from 6:00 P.M. - midnight. These are simply suggestions and can be used as a good guide when figuring out your own timeline. You should receive a banquet event order (BEO) from your caterer or venue listing the timeline of events, including dinner and other important details of your reception. You always want to make sure that your timeline, your venue's timeline, and your DJ/band's timeline is one in the same. It is very important that everyone is on the same page and knows what and when something is supposed to happen.

6:00 P.M. - 7:00 P.M. - Cocktails and Hors d'oeuvres - This is a great time to have a receiving line so you can greet guests as they arrive and then you don't have to visit each table during dinner. A receiving line includes you and your spouse and both sets of parents. There is no reason for anyone else to be a part of it; unless of course you need a sibling explaining to you who each guest is. Or, does that just happen at ridiculously ginormous Italian weddings?

You might want to arrive at your reception site a little earlier than the start time. This is the perfect opportunity for you and your new husband to view the reception space before anyone else comes in. Take a moment to really look and see that all of your planning finally paid off. You worked so hard on designing those centerpieces or picking just the right linens. Take it all in because once your guests enter that room, it'll never be the same. And it gives you a moment alone to just breathe. . . .and maybe do a shot... I mean, glamorously sip champagne.

7:00 P.M. - 7:30 P.M. - DJ/Emcee begin to make introductions. Introductions happen in the same order as your ceremony processional. The cake cutting is next. You might as well walk right to the cake and cut it. The cake is usually displayed in the middle of your dance floor so the sooner the venue staff can take it away, the better! Speeches will happen after the cake cutting and begin with the best man, then the maid of honor, and concluded by the father of the bride.

7:30 P.M. - 9:00 P.M. - Dinner. You have an hour and a half here. Do something with it. Maybe sit and eat and enjoy being Mr. & Mrs.!

9:00 P.M. - midnight - Cocktails and dancing.

A couple of things that need to be included throughout the evening, if you are choosing to have them, the first dance, the mother/son dance, and the father/bride dance. The first dance can take place as soon as the two of you are introduced into the room. If a half hour doesn't seem like enough time to get through the introductions, cake cutting, and speeches, spread them out during dinner. You can also get up during one of the courses to either cut the cake or have the first dance. In addition to breaking-up dinner a little bit, it provides some entertainment for your guests. Besides, at this point everyone is still sitting, enjoying the meal, so they will actually pay attention while still somewhat sober! You may also want to have the father/daughter dance and mother/son dance during dinner courses as well. You usually have at least an hour and a half for just dinner; so, I highly suggest incorporating as much as you can during that time. Then you can enjoy the rest of the evening with your guests and not worry about anything else! After dinner is the perfect time to have the bouquet and garter toss, if you're even having them.

Make it fun and make it your own!

GOD NOOO!!! THE SEATING CHART

UGH! I think this is seriously the *most* dreaded part of the entire wedding planning process! It can make or break a marriage, before the actual marriage. Between remembering which family member doesn't talk to the other and what friends would or don't get along . . . and then there's always that one person who comes alone and might not know anyone (seriously? just send a fricken' card . . . with money! Kidding...but am I?) . . . who can keep up? Oh, and then if your parents are divorced, *Good lawd, forget about it!* A complete nightmare. Wouldn't it be amazing if just for one night, everyone could actually act like adults and get along for the sake of you and your spouse?! Oh, a girl can dream. And for the people who can't, I am looking down and judging you.

The best advice I can give here is to put on your favorite music, open up your favorite bottle of wine (or vodka), write out each guest's name on those colored tab post its, have round paper plates on hand with table numbers written on them, and just start posting away. This will allow you to move names around until you are comfortable with where everyone is sitting. Or you get completely drunk and just don't give a shit anymore. It's a win-win! If that doesn't work, this might be one situation where more opinions are better than none. Ask close friends and family members for help.

Obviously the seating chart is one of the last pieces of the wedding planning puzzle. You can't complete this task until you have the final number of guests attending. Once you have all of this information, ask for a diagram of the room from your venue. They can usually help you with the setup and know how many tables you will need for your final number, as well as how many tables will fit in the room. If they don't offer this information and it is up to you to figure it out, please read below. (A little side note. If you are having children at your reception, it might be a good idea to have a kid's table after dinner and provide them with coloring books or other fun activities they can do together).

One way to stay organized is to start a spreadsheet for the meals. This will be extremely helpful if you're offering a meal choice to your guests, especially for wait staff. You will undoubtedly have vegetarians or people who are gluten free or have an allergy of some kind; so, the spreadsheet will be a great tool for the servers to deliver the proper meal to the proper tables. Take special note of the table(s) at which your parents are seated because it's a big day for them as well and the wait staff likes to take extra special care of them.

If you are giving your guests a meal option, indicate their meal selection on the place card. This is another way to help the wait staff deliver the correct meal to each person.

For example: Add a little colored dot in the corner or back of place cards with red indicating meat, yellow indicating chicken, and blue indicating fish.

Below is an example of how to create a spreadsheet and floorplan based on the meal selections.

WEDDING NAME/ DATE OF WEDDING

TABLES	Chicken	Beef	Fish	Kid	Veg/Vegan	Comments	Total
HEAD TABLE	4	6					10
TABLE 1	4	4		2		Parents of the Bride	10
TABLE 2	3	5					8
TABLE 3	3	6			1	Vegan Meal	10
TABLE 4	7		2			Gluten allergy	9
TABLE 5		10					10
TABLE 6	3	6	1			Parents of the Groom	10
TABLE 7	4		4	2			10
TABLE 8		7			2	Vegetarian	9
TABLE 9	3	6	1				10
TABLE 10	4					Vendor Table	4
TOTAL	35	50	8	4	3		100
TOTAL	Chicken	Beef	Fish	Kids	Veg/Vegan		

Basically, you want to just list the number of tables and meal options, and simply fill in the blanks with your guest's choices. Don't forget to include yourself and your spouse in the final count, as well as your vendors if they are having a meal! For some reason, every time I am sitting with my clients as we finalize numbers, they *never* seem to add up! The seating chart numbers somehow don't match the number of meals . . . and it's a mad panic to figure this out! I don't know why this happens, but it does. It's better to sort it all out the week of the wedding and not the day of. The more organized you are, the better. More often than not part of the mystery is solved because the bride and groom forget to include themselves in the final count.

When creating your floorplan, I would put the table number and the amount of people at each table. This way, staff will have the correct amount of chairs and place settings for that table. Below is an example of this. Again, just another way for your numbers to not add up correctly. *So. Frustrating.*

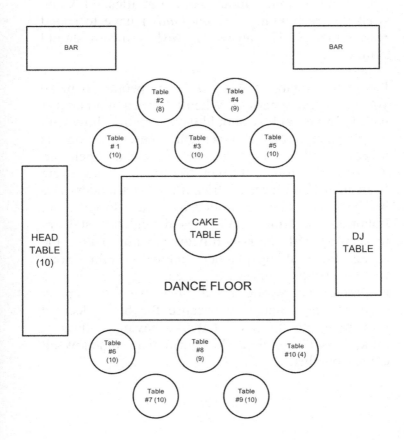

FINAL PAYMENTS AND GRATUITIES

Most if not all of your vendors and venue will require final payment the week of the wedding. This is also a good time to think about extra gratuities. I know what you're thinking: *Oh my God*, I have to spend *more* money?! The answer is *yes*! And you should want to!

Please understand it takes *a lot* of people to make your perfect day perfect. When I worked at a banquet hall, I always said we should have a reality show with a split screen of the reception where everyone is laughing and dancing, enjoying the music, open bar, and delicious food, and then the reality of the event from behind the scenes. Imagine the bartenders and bar backs are running around like crazy to get more liquor and cut lemons and limes, the culinary staff try to keep up with the hors d'oeuvres while plating the salads, the wedding planner frantically ladling soup for the soup course while realizing the chef is preparing the wrong salad! The banquet captain searching high and low because the bride decided right then and there she felt like having a glass of milk. It is a complete shit storm that somehow all comes together.

With that said, additional tipping is something you should try to incorporate into your wedding-planning budget. Before making a list of everyone you have to tip, read contracts and make sure gratuities are included with all vendors. If they aren't, you want to be sure to set a little aside for them. If gratuity is included in the contract, anything above their gratuity is completely at your own discretion. If you feel your vendors did an exceptional job for you, it is always appreciated to be recognized for their work and a very nice gesture on your end.

Here is a list of people to keep in mind when distributing tips:

1. Hairstylist and Makeup Artist - this is expected. Standard is 20% - 25% based on their quality of service.

2. Ceremony Officiant - If you are having the ceremony at your church and you are charged to use the space or required to give a "suggested donation," it's not necessary to tip anything extra. Altar servers are typically tipped $10 each. If you are having an offsite officiant, consider giving him/her an additional $50-$100.

3. Ceremony Musicians - This is optional and not required. If they did amazing work, $10 - $20 per musician is acceptable.

4. Band or DJ - This is not expected, however, if you'd like to give them something extra, $20 or so per musician in the band is the norm. Gratuity for the DJ can be anywhere from $50 - $150.

5. Transportation – Limo and trolley drivers. Tip about 15 - 20% of the total bill.

6. Reception Staff - Gratuity is almost always built into your contract, however, if you feel the banquet manager, servers, bartenders, or anyone else helping in the room were attentive and really treated you and your guests well, tip them whatever you're comfortable giving. Trust me, anything they receive, will be appreciated.

7. Reception Attendants - This includes bathroom and coatroom attendants and valet parking staff. These people most likely will not be part of the gratuities and tipping will be well received. Consider $1 per guest or per car for valet and a set amount for the bathroom staff about $50 or so.

8. Delivery and Setup Staff - Think of everyone coming in that day to deliver the furnishings and fixtures. Those who deliver the flowers, wedding cake, sound systems, lighting, tents, chairs, and porta potties should be tipped approximately $5 - $10 per person.

9. Photographer/Videographer - This is completely optional and usually not expected. However, if your particular photographers do not own the studio and they really did a great job, consider giving them something extra $50 - $150 each.

10. Wedding Planner - Again, this is optional. A thank you card, photos from the wedding of their work, or a small gift to show your appreciation is very kind. Let's be honest, I've never met a wedding planner, or anyone for that matter, who turned down cold hard cash.

Most of the payments and tipping will be taken care of throughout the night or at the end of the evening. Usually the best man or groomsmen will be in charge of passing out the envelopes for payment and gratuity to each person. Otherwise, if your wedding planner is on-site throughout your entire reception, they can usually handle it. But, remember to assign someone the task. The bride might want to give the wedding planner the payment and gratuity so she can express her appreciation one last time.

~PERSONAL STORY~

The Generous Bride

I once had a bride who took $20 cash out of every paycheck and built a wedding tip envelope.

How smart is that! This allowed her to have her tip money set aside by the time the wedding date arrived. All she had to do was divvy it up. Instead of stressing the week of the wedding when all of her final payments were due or frantically opening envelopes at the end of the night searching for cash, she was extremely prepared. She and her fiancé were on a tight budget, as they were paying for almost everything themselves. So, this worked very well for them.

Learn from the generous bride and make adjustments for what works for you and plan ahead. There's never harm in pre-planning, especially when it comes to budgeting.

Formalwear

Guys, go pick up the tuxedos you hopefully ordered a few months ago. I warned you!

Steam your dress

The bridal shop will steam and set your dress for you. All you will have to do is unwrap it and let it sit in an elevated position where it can breathe.

Change your name

If you are planning on changing your surname, this can actually be done any time. I hear it's kind of a pain in the ass, so might as well get it out of the way.

Personal care

Manicure and pedicure - Grab your girls and have a fun day! Or, if you're on a tighter budget, the night before the wedding make your own spa at home with your bridesmaids. It would be a great cost efficient way to bring everyone together to de-stress and have fun! And, hopefully someone knows how to paint nails. Don't forget your haircut, color, and wax if needed.

Reception duties

If you do not have an on-site planner or DOC, you will want to delegate reception duties to friends and family members. For example, who will set up the places cards, favors, or gift table?

Rehearsal Dinner

The rehearsal dinner will take place a night or two before the wedding. This is traditionally planned and paid for by the parents of the groom. This is a great time for your bridal party and those participating in your wedding to unwind, relax, and just have fun altogether. It is also customary to invite your out-of-town guests to the rehearsal dinner. At this time you will give your bridal party and parents the gifts you purchased for everyone.

CHAPTER CHECKLIST

_____ Confirm with all vendors (this is something your wedding planner will do if you have hired one)

_____ Give final guest count

_____ Provide seating chart

_____ Ceremony checklist

_____ Reception checklist

_____ Hotel check list

_____ Make final payments and organize
      additional gratuities

_____ Pick up formalwear for men

_____ Steam your dress

_____ Change name

_____ Personal care

_____ Delegate reception duties if you do not have
      a wedding planner.

_____ Rehearsal dinner

Chapter 8

Name . . . That . . . BRIDE!!!!

Here is a little fun fact based on my experiences: almost every single couple gets engaged around the holidays (between November and February). December is the most popular month to pop the question. June has always been the most popular month for a wedding; however, July and August are quickly on June's tail. September and October weddings are also rising, most likely due to milder weather. Winter months and early spring are generally considered off season, meaning better deals and pricing. With that said, weddings take place all year round so it is important to bring up a very serious topic: Bridezillas!

I want you all to understand there is nothing fun or cute about being a bridezilla, except maybe the kind of cute creative name for a nightmare bride. I realize television has glamorized this type of behavior by making it funny to boost ratings; but, I promise you there is nothing funny about it. Not to mention, if anyone truly has to deal with such a bride, I question how she has friends and more importantly how in the hell did she land a fiancé?

I can honestly say in 10 years of planning weddings, I have never worked with a bridezilla . . . momzilla, that's a different story! Mothers, let's not live vicariously through our daughters and force them, because you're paying, to have the wedding we never did! But I digress.

I think the best thing I can do for you here is simply list completely unacceptable, like borderline, psycho behavior. Let's be honest, your wedding is not going down in the history books and it's certainly not going to be any different than the hundreds of other weddings I've planned. This I guarantee you. What will make your wedding different are *you* and your *groom*. This is your chance to show off your personalities, style, and most importantly, the friendship and love between you and your significant other.

Important reminder: I've said it before and I'll say it again. *You are not the first person to get married.*

Think very long and hard about the way you decide to treat people involved, like your parents, siblings, your bridal party, vendors, and everyone else who you encounter. I'd also quickly like to point out, once engaged, it should be "our" wedding, never "my" wedding. Brides oftentimes plan weddings as "mine," and forget to include the groom. Remember ladies, there would be no wedding without your man so don't make him question his decision. Set a good, happy, upbeat, I'm so excited to marry you tone from the beginning. Don't let him see your true colors until after the "I do." Hahaha, but seriously, successful marriages are teams; so, let's plan as a team (and guess what, guys love sports references so let him know this is a team effort).

Let's start by saying you have no right to set ground rules for anyone involved in your wedding. You are not doing anyone a favor by asking them to stand up in your wedding. I was truly honored each and every time I was asked to stand up in one of my best friends or family members' weddings. I knew it would be a fun and memorable experience that I was excited to be a part of. However, if any of them started dictating how my life was going to be lived the entire year leading up to *their* big day; I would have bowed out gracefully or sat and had a long conversation before destroying any lifelong friendships.

I have read and heard about some very tragic behavior that takes place between brides and her maids and I'm not sure if I should laugh because it can't possibly be true or set them straight because they need to clearly be brought down a notch. Below is a list of no-nos that every bride should avoid at all costs.

List of HUGE no nos

1. Weekly weigh-ins and/or the request that no one is skinnier than the bride. This is a contradictory statement. Do you want me to be skinny? Or, just at a reasonable weight of your choosing?

2. The demand to cover-up tattoos. Ah, ok...so should I get them lasered off or is covering them up good enough for you?

3. Enforcing no haircuts and/or dye jobs leading up to the wedding unless it is okayed by the bride. But why?

4. Forbidding anyone in your bridal party to get pregnant before the wedding. Yes, why would I even think of something as menial as starting my family when you are getting married?

5. Vacations during wedding planning. This is your wedding, right?

6. Suggesting bridesmaids can't afford your wedding, like suggesting the dress might be too expensive for them or they can't afford to attend a bachelorette party. Are we even friends?

7. Expecting family and friends who live out of town to be at every wedding festivity you decide to throw. Will you be paying their way into town for each event?

8. Threatening to kick someone out of the bridal party for not following the rules. Do you even like any of us?

9. Telling people to cancel life plans from the time you get engaged to the time you walk down the aisle. This includes, but not limited to, illnesses, vacations, emergencies of any kind, and lastly family deaths. I will make damn sure no one dies on my watch while you are planning your wedding.

10. Referring to you as anyone's "Boss." This will most likely not be well received.

11. Implying any of them can easily be substituted and replaced. Clearly our special bond can never be broken...oh...wait.

12. Sending a weekly email of wedding-planning updates and expecting a prompt response from everyone. *No one cares.*

13. Having a 12-page detailed "fun" wedding agenda the week of the wedding, followed by a *Cliff's Notes* version and extensive timeline of events the actual day of the wedding. No one is following it. . . not even you. . . believe me. Let it go and you will be far less stressed the day of.

If you find any of the above acceptable, I don't know what to say, except good luck to your fiancé. Putting a ring on your finger does not give you a free pass to be an absolute nut job nor dictate and control a person's life while you've temporarily (hopefully) lost your sanity.

~ Personal Story~

The Beyond Bitch Bride

Another wedding planner and personal friend once worked with a major bridezilla. She was awful to everyone: her parents, her planner, fiancé, vendors, and was especially hard on her six bridesmaids. So hard on them, in fact, that one stepped down half way through while another purposely forgot the bride's overnight bag she was supposed to bring to the hotel.

It all started when she told the girls at the initial dress fitting that dresses will not be ordered over a specific size and that she picked her most important skinny friends, because who wants fat people in their wedding pictures? Her bridezilla tendencies continued as she behaved in the following ways (seriously):

She picked everyone's shoe and nail color; the day of the wedding, she made one girl switch her hair because it was too similar to the bride's own style; she told another to have her makeup done over because, in her opinion, it wasn't good enough; she didn't like one of the girl's husbands, but told her it was ok to bring him; one wasn't allowed to bring her boyfriend because he just didn't fit in with her wedding guests. It didn't end there.

Of course, every girl was given a simple job to help set up the reception. And so began the retaliation. One gal was to scatter these little crystals around the centerpiece. She was scolded (yes, scolded . . . a grown woman scolded by her friend) and told it had to be redone. Another got so drunk at the wedding reception she reamed the bride in the bathroom, with a few guests present, and then told her she was no longer a bridesmaid in her own wedding. I could keep going . . . but it's too painful. I just don't understand this type of behavior. What are you looking to gain here?

Let's remember what kind of bride you should strive to be—happy, stress free, polite, and appreciative. One that will enjoy her day with her new spouse, family, and friends. Do not be a tabloid's dream bride. Seriously. Don't be a bitch.

Social Media Star- In Her Mind

Social media has become a huge part of society and the media apps are great for so many reasons; such as staying connected to family and friends who live out of state, supporting local businesses, stalking your friend's new crush, or killing hours of your down time by looking through photos. Hours of your life you'll never get back. Hours, that on this day are much better spent with friends and family who are just as excited to spend this day with you as you are with them.

So *please* put down your phone. *Live* in the moment and really be *present.*

With that being said, some couples believe that their wedding isn't complete without a customized hashtag A hashtag is a way to tag photos on social media. Using a hashtag allows you to easily search and collect photos taken by your wedding guests. Couples can promote their hashtags on their wedding websites.

Many couples opt into creating websites to keep guests informed about the details of the big day. Most customized wedding websites include the following: the story of how the couple met; a photo gallery; introduction of the bridal party; registry links; location of the wedding and reception; overnight accommodations, which is especially helpful for out-of-town guests; and, of course, a countdown to the "I dos."

Now that your wedding hashtag and website have been created, you're ready to document the entire day on social media. This is a great opportunity for your bridal party to really get involved. Encourage your bridal party and guests to capture the magic of your special moments while you enjoy the company of people who are important in your life. It's important for you to actually be in the moment. Remember that.

There will be plenty of people excited to take a picture and post it, all the while using your super creative wedding hashtag, So, I can guarantee you not a single moment will be missed. Oh yeah and let's not forget the thousands of dollars you've just spent on that *professional* photographer who certainly is not interested in taking a photo of you and your hubby on your phones. Your wedding day is not the time to bury yourself in social media. You will have plenty of time after the wedding to scroll through and relive the moments during which you were creating the first memories of being Mr. and Mrs.

~ Personal Story~

The Cloud...wait is that a cloud 9 Bride

This story is about the importance of truly being in the moment.

I once had a bride who wanted it to look like she was dancing on a cloud during her first dance. What a fairy tale like image! The DJ brought in a fog machine. As the music started, the bride and her new husband walked to the center of the dance floor, rather than celebrating the fact that she was dancing for the first time with her husband, she just kept looking around her feet to make sure the fog seemed like a cloud. *Come. On*! I don't think she once looked at the groom. I'm sure it made for lovely pictures. I promise no one left thinking WOW! I too want to dance on a cloud! No one cared.

They probably didn't even realize what was going on aside from wondering why they could hardly breathe due to so much darn fog in the air.

Live in the moment. Experience the moment. Do not consume yourself with small details that people undoubtedly won't notice or care about.

DIY . . . Oh no you didn't

I'm going to share with you a couple of things websites...where you pin things... have taught me. I am not a baker, an artist, seamstress, makeup artist (learned that one the hard way), hair stylist, and definitely not a painter. In fact, I'm not crafty at all.

Now, deep down inside I always knew I didn't possess any sort of hidden raw talent, which would eventually burst through once a DIY website showed me the 16 "simple" steps of turning my boyfriend's old sweater into a scarf. But yet it sucks me in *Every. Single. Time.*

I can't help but click on a new do it yourself project, inevitably resulting in an epic fail. This leads me to our topic: The Do-It-Yourself Bride.

Yes ladies, in theory this sounds like a glorious idea. This allows the ability to not only save money, but really make it your own by showing off your personality through your crazy good art skills you never knew you had . . . and probably don't. Having your bridal party come over to hot glue every little thing they can paste fake jewels on is not a work of art. I'm here to tell you this is a BAD idea. Unless you have the skill and know how to create incredible projects that would make the craftiest of women jealous, I'd put down the magic markers and hire a professional.

Don't get me wrong, there are plenty of things you can easily do yourself, like anything that involves a computer and ink. Place cards, for example, or programs for your ceremony, and save the dates are easy DIYs. You get the picture. Want to make them fun? Paste a little rhinestone or something in the corner. Or, a fun seating chart idea includes old window panes that you can write guest's names on.

Make sure you have good handwriting. You can create cute little signs for the guest book or sweet table. Centerpieces that involve detailed flower arrangements, if you're not a florist, may not be the best idea.

Delegating or divide and conquering are a great way for your bridal party to help you out with little details. Spending every night at your house for one week tying tiny blue bows and gluing them on a wedding program is not delegating. It's obnoxious. Instead, invite everyone over to help stuff and stamp your wedding invitations. Or maybe you need to put the table numbers into picture frames or have someone pin a ribbon around your unity candle for your church ceremony. These are acceptable delegated tasks. If you don't want to spend the time on a meticulous DIY project, don't think for a second that anyone else wants to either. Bring wine . . . not a glue gun.

~ Personal Story~
The Bedazzled Bride

I once had an over the top do-it-yourselfer bride. I mean, she literally made everything herself! The week of the wedding I have brides bring all of their decorations to me: favors, place cards, cake topper, cake knife and server, etc., to ensure all items are checked off the list and not forgotten. Well, to my surprise, she made everything from centerpieces and favors to chair covers (I'm not kidding . . . she f'ing sewed chair covers *WTF!*), as well as little signs with adorable love quotes awkwardly painted on them.

While I appreciated her enthusiasm and effort, I knew this was going to be a disaster. The day of the wedding as I am beginning to set up her reception, I went to get the items she had brought to me. All of them were stuck together—no joke! I was pulling off construction paper from places I'm not even sure it belonged. She made a sign for the sweet table with huge letters spelling out her new last name attached to a wood base. Each letter took a serious nosedive. I spent a good two hours gluing, stapling, and praying everything would come together . . . or at least look like it did. Glue guns actually can be your friend in time of crisis. In the end, she came in, looked around and asked if I put the white rose petals on the place card table? I did. Mind you these were fake white rose petals that she wanted on a white tablecloth . . . not sure how she missed them?! She then turned to me and with a huge hug said everything looked perfect (with absolutely no help from the do-it-yourself bride).

Just remember, unless you are a professional in all areas of your wedding, it will most likely wind up costing you more money, frustration, and stress that is completely unnecessary. If not for yourself, definitely for your wedding planner! You want your wedding to look elegant and timeless, not like a kindergarten art project, right? So gals, put down the be-dazzler, remember the amazing talents you do have, and stick with those. No pun intended.

Chapter 9
Speeches - Because everyone needs a little help

I realize this chapter would be more helpful to the people you've chosen to actually give the speeches, so maybe you should highlight and have all of them read it.

It is considered an honor to be asked to deliver a speech at a wedding; but, giving a speech can be tricky. People worry about the length of the speech, the appropriateness of the content, and, not to mention, the fear of public speaking.

While many people continue to give traditional speeches, it seems nowadays they include either an elaborate choreographed dance number or full out rap medley performed by the bridesmaids that is recorded and put on YouTube. This can be really cool if you remember to keep it about the bride and groom and not focus on your five minutes of fame. I guess people do not fear speaking and or performing in public anymore?

Here are a couple of helpful tips to stay on track when writing your speech.

DOs OF WEDDING SPEECHES

1. Actually write a speech and practice it before show time.

2. Include personal anecdotes that most, if not all, guests can relate to; including specific details about the couple.

3. Try to memorize your speech so that you can actually look at the couple while speaking and not reading off a piece of paper.

4. Carry index cards to help stay on track.

5. Try to add tasteful humor. Make it interesting and keep it fun!

6. Ideally the speech should be no more than 3 - 5 minutes.

7. Keep the tone upbeat and enthusiastic.

8. Personalize it. You were chosen to give a speech for a reason, so celebrate the special relationship you have with the couple.

9. Stand while giving the speech.

10. Don't forget to toast and congratulate the couple!

DONT'S OF WEDDING SPEECHES

1. Don't make the speech about you. Introduce yourself, explain the relationship to the couple, but leave out the drawn out history of life events. No one needs to know you sold Girl Scout cookies together.

2. Do not talk about past relationships (ex-boyfriends or girlfriends). Even if the story is so funny to you and the bride, it won't be funny that day.

3. Do not mention sad events. Including illnesses, deaths, or past break ups. If the couple wants to honor someone who is no longer with them, they will find a way to do it.

4. Do not try to embarrass the couple by telling personal stories that are distasteful and inappropriate.

5. Inside personal jokes are great! Leave them out of your speech. No one gets it but you.

6. If you want to talk about a personal experience you've shared but aren't sure if they would appreciate it, run it by the couple to make sure they're comfortable with it. On second thought, if you're questioning it, I'd probably leave it out.

7. Don't mumble.

8. Don't get drunk before giving your speech . . . maybe one shot to take the edge off, but that's it!

9. Do not carry a drink with you while speaking.

10. Do not improvise. If you lose track of your thoughts, do not start rambling. Find a way to end the speech.

Oftentimes speeches are a wedding planner's worst enemy. We try to stick to a pretty tight timeline during dinner to ensure your guests are not sitting any longer than they have to with only table wine to drink. Especially the "we didn't know where else to put these people" table way in the back where nobody knows anyone they're sitting with. Unfortunately, most people are more concerned with the open bar than they are anything else. Not to mention, the longer the timeline is thrown off, the longer your meals sit in a hot box . . . making them not so tasty.

With that said, couples, when planning your timeline for the reception, figure out how much time is given for speeches. Typically, the maid of honor and best man will toast you two, as well as a mother or father of the bride and groom or a close family member. I would try to stick with that and not ask every single one of your friends and siblings to say a little something. However, if your list of speech givers is growing and you can't tell any of them no, then try spreading them out throughout dinner and not have them all speak at one time. This way, dinner can start as planned and it breaks it up a little bit! And, newlyweds please remember to stand up and give a little speech of your own, thanking guests for coming and everyone else who made this day possible.

I also try to make it a rule with the couple and the DJ or band that the only speeches given are those noted in your timeline. Once dancing begins, the microphone is off limits. It's not drunk karaoke time, and Uncle Bob does not need to sing happy birthday to himself . . . again.

An open mic can become a hot mess and disruptive to your dance party, honestly. Unless someone gets special permission from the bride or groom, I recommend the mic stays off and out of reach.

~ Personal Story ~

Long Story Longer

A little story about how speeches (and a bad wedding planner) can throw things off a bit. I once attended a wedding, I'm pretty sure just about everyone in attendance decided to "say a little something". During speech number two, they served the salad . . . awesome, dinner will continue! Oh, no, no. By speech number six, the dirty salad plate was still sitting in front of me and an hour and a half later (yes, I timed it—I'm a wedding planner for Christ's sake), I am still waiting for my main course. This just isn't right. Not only from a planner's point of view, but for your guests as well. The planner should have made the decision to keep dinner moving along, or at the very least asked the wait staff to clear the empty salad plates. The guests at my table were complaining so badly, that I asked the wedding planner if she could perhaps take away the dirty plates. A reasonable request, I thought. She did. And then went and told the bride and groom I complained! Extremely unprofessional. To this day I don't understand her need to tell them. What was the point...of you?

Hmmm...I guess I'm still harboring some feelings of anger toward the planner. Point is, try to keep your speeches to a minimum. Regardless, in the end the wedding was beautiful and we all had a great time.

Chapter 10

Brides that took the plunge - what would they change?

I think it's great for current or future brides to hear what past brides would have done differently. Been there, done that, and what they would have changed. I surveyed 100 past brides; just kidding . . . who has time to read all those emails? I simply asked the question on social media and my former brides as well as my married friends were eager to share their experiences. I found it interesting that many had the same ideas and feeling about what they would have changed. I sincerely couldn't agree more with all these comments. They are honest and true and definitely something worth thinking about.

Due to legal purposes, I did not use real names . . . not sure if you could tell?

Smarty Smarterson Bride:

In retrospect, I think there are certainly some things I'd have done differently:

> • Let others handle things more; not even delegating so much as just letting go of control with some things (bachelor/ette party).

> • If it won't break the bank, spring for what you want. I still regret that we didn't get a photo booth for the reception--love those, and they're so inexpensive now!

• Don't let yourself get caught up with planning an aspect that you're indifferent about. If you don't have a vision for the centerpieces or bouquets, go with what's simple and tasteful and move on.

• Don't take on more than you can handle. We can all be super women when we need to, but it can make the days and weeks leading up to the wedding more stressful than they have to be.

Woulda Shoulda Coulda Bride

I would say don't put yourself in debt over a "party." My husband and I were pretty budget minded. We gave ourselves a number and stuck to it, but sh*t adds up! Seriously, at the end of the day it's about you and your significant other. It's not about the dress, hair/makeup, what the guys wear, or even the fancy monograms and lighting; it's about the two of you. People get so wrapped-up in the other stuff. If I had to do it over again, I would have gone to city hall and then spent the money on an amazing honeymoon instead of a weekend resort in Michigan. We promised ourselves Hawaii at five years of marriage. Well, then kids came along and life happened. So five years later I'm still staring at the damn brochure!

Passive Bride

Definitely stress less. I definitely wish I hadn't focused so much on making everyone else happy, sometimes at the expense of what I wanted. I also let some vendors talk me into things, flowers for example, and I should have stuck to my guns a little more. You can probably see a little trend of people pleasing here, but I have to imagine I'm not the only one who does that. While I'm not suggesting say F everyone and their thoughts, but it really is the couple's day. That's really about it, actually; I loved our wedding and reception.

I LOVED my Wedding Bride

The things you think you "need" for the wedding are probably not going to matter when everything is done. Save yourself the money. Also, just elope. Bad answer?

Me and My Hubby Bride

Don't let anyone influence your decisions—it's your day. And it's about you and your future spouse; so, don't worry about pleasing everyone else.

Know What She Wants Bride

Less is more; stick to what you want, not another's opinions. Focus on the real point of that day. Do you want a party or a marriage, which one is supposed to last? Let the man be involved, as much or as little as he wants, it's his day too. Spend money on the photos, that's what you take with you forever.

Realistic Bride

I think that the last piece of advice this generation of brides needs to hear is that it is not all about them. A marriage is about the two of you, your extended family, and your friends who are important to both of you. If you forget that, good luck getting beyond year two.

Picture This Bride

I would have done more research on my photographers. I like my pictures but I'm not in love with them. Those pictures are memories that you will have forever so make sure you find a good one.

What Happens in Vegas Bride

We got married in Vegas. Best. Decision. Ever. We saved money. It was what *we* wanted. People loved it. It was fun and different. What you think is important and matters *so much* right now won't matter years later. After two kids and eleven years of marriage, I am so happy we didn't spend a boatload of money on our wedding. We have needed and used the money for more important things over the years. Oh and also, I promise you - *no one* will remember or keep the favor you gave out, the place card, or the huge center pieces; so, try not to go crazy in spending on that stuff.

Perfect Perspective Bride

Smaller is better. People were at my wedding I didn't even know. If I had to do it over again, I would have done a small, less traditional wedding somewhere with our closest friends and family, focusing more on the day and less on everything else. I had a wonderful day, but regret not spending more intimate time with the people who really are the most important in my life.

Makes Sense to Me Bride

Weddings are often the biggest and best party you'll ever plan. If you make it all about you, you'll leave your guests in the dust. Later in life as your perspective changes a bit, you don't want to think back to that day and remember that you were an overly self-centered bridezilla at the expense of your guests, family, and friends. In addition, you'll stress yourself out because if any little thing goes wrong, it will ruin your day. If the wedding is all about you, the problem is your problem. If you can step away from it a little bit, it will make it so much easier to sit back and enjoy the day without getting overwhelmed by any bumps in the road. Being yourselves, making memories, and having fun with the people you love – that is what is important.

The Wedding Planner Bride

I find with this DIY generation of brides, a lot of my brides looking back would have either done less DIY projects for their wedding or delegated more. A lot of them try to do everything themselves and a lot ends up being last minute or not what they thought it was going to be, and this just adds to their stress level. I outsourced everything because I had the connections and I knew better. Ha!

I think some past brides would have changed their mentality from more is more to less is more. You know how some brides need the linens, the overlay, the runners, three different centerpieces, chiavari chairs, and chair bows. I feel like a lot of them look back and realize that covering already provided banquet chairs, an overlay over provided linens, and a simple classic centerpiece can work just as well. That would have left them more money for their honeymoon. I feel like a lot of brides don't actually budget for the honeymoon and just hope that they get a ton of cash in their cards. Not a good idea.

So what everyone was trying to say here is *hire a wedding planner.* . . Call me!

~ Personal Story~
5 Years Too Long

I was in a relationship for five-plus years and I was so anxious for him to put a ring on my finger. Not because I wanted to spend the rest of my life with the guy, but because we had been together for so long that I thought it should just be the next step, right? And honestly, every single one of my girlfriends was getting engaged and some of them hadn't even been together as long as the two of us. It didn't matter that I would wake up on certain days in a panic and tell him I didn't want to get married (he was like, I didn't ask ...*whatever* rude!) or think to myself this can't be all there is to life. Ladies, if you have these thoughts, don't do it! Long story short, we did finally break up and many of my friends who had gotten married unfortunately ended in divorce . . . or they should be divorced, in my opinion. So, if you know it isn't right, it will be extremely difficult to walk away, but in the long run you will be so much happier. Trust me; life is so much better being single and happy than being in a not so happy relationship.

If you are having any second thoughts, it will be far more expensive to get a divorce than to call off your wedding. It is so important to remember that. Be sure you are making the right decision for the right reasons; the marriage and not the idea of marriage, or the party, or the ring. Unless the ring is ridiculously big and beautiful and looks really expensive ... then maybe you can work it out?

Ask yourself the serious questions like, how old am I? How much money does he make? How good looking is he? How good do we look together? So what if he doesn't know the difference between their, there, and they're? That was a test! If you are asking yourself any of these questions and honestly contemplating the answers to them to get you down the aisle, just walk away.

Chapter 11

What have we learned here?

Now that we have a pretty good timeline to work from to get you successfully down the aisle, let's recap some pretty important information along with a few personal stories . . . as I like to always keep things in perspective.

Your wedding is *One. Day.*

- This is *one* day of your life. You do not need to spend a fortune. People will remember two things. First, the food; if you're Italian it's the only thing your guests will remember so make it good and have a lot of it. And for everyone else, second is the open bar!

- Remember to enjoy the engagement period before jumping into planning. Take time to bask in the lovey-dovey bliss of your new status as a soon-to-be married couple. Start thinking about your wedding about twelve months out and plan your budget. Hire a wedding planner.

- Research vendors and remember that *everything* is negotiable. Vendors need your business as much as you need them. Don't be afraid to negotiate! Be willing to compromise. Don't stress and overspend on small details *no one* will notice but you. Do you really need

Swavorski crystals on your pedicure when you're wearing closed toe shoes? The more open you are to hearing ideas from your vendors and wedding planner, the more likely you will find sensible solutions.

~ **Personal Story~**

The My Way Only Bride

I worked with a couple who wanted their 120-person wedding on Labor Day weekend at a specific hotel. There was no compromising. The room they wanted held a much larger number of people and required a much larger minimum revenue than what is typically expected of a wedding that size. I spoke with their on-site coordinator to figure out a way to make this work. Fortunately, we were able to include their rehearsal dinner and their morning after breakfast in minimum revenue and meet the financial requirement. This worked out only because the hotel didn't have anything booked the evening before or the morning after. If you are planning on having multiple events at one location you will have more room to negotiate. Tell your venue exactly what you want and ask how they can make that happen. You have nothing to lose!

- If you are going to have a theme to your wedding be sure to keep it tasteful and remember it is a reflection of you and your soon-to-be hubby's personal style.

- Remember to have realistic expectations of your bridal party and everyone else involved in your wedding planning. When thinking about pre-and post-wedding events take into consideration the time and money others have dedicated to you over the last year.

- As the big day quickly approaches, remember not to stress the small stuff.

~ Personal Story~

It's literally the same exact dress!

One of my close friends, whose wedding I was standing up in, asked if I wanted to come see the two dresses she was considering. Yes, I would love to! She was a bit stressed out because she loved them both and couldn't decide between the two and just did not know what to do. As her mother and I were sitting in the room, she came out in dress number one, and it was beautiful. She looked perfect. It was the dress for her, no question. I kept my opinion to myself because I knew we had another one to evaluate.

When she came out in dress number two, I was a bit confused. I could have *sworn* it was the same dress as number one? I'm not kidding, I think the only difference might have been one--and I mean *one* tiny little bead . . . maybe. She became hysterical because how was she possibly going to make this decision? I knew I had to be serious because she was so shaken up, but all I really wanted to do was laugh and scream, *they are the same f'ing dress!* In the end, she chose number one and never looked back at number two, which had one extra bead . . . maybe. Do not get caught up in the small stuff that literally no one will notice!

- Talk to other brides and see what they loved and what they would change about their weddings. Learning from others can save you a lot of stress in the long run.

- Remember to unplug from social media and be in the moment. After all, you only have one wedding day (We hope. But, I'll be happy to help you plan number two!).

- At no time are you permitted to be a bridezilla. Ever. I'm not kidding. Ever

Planning your wedding can be stressful. For that reason, I have created a list of daily wedding planning affirmations to help ground you during stressful times.

Your Daily Wedding Planning Affirmations

1. I promise to stress less!

2. I *will* prioritize!

3. I promise to be organized!

4. I will make an effort to spend money wisely. This will not be the wedding to end all weddings . . . unless I win the lottery, then really, who cares!

5. I really understand the true meaning of the day. It's about me and my fiancé!

6. Less is actually more!

7. This is *one day* in my life. .

8. I will be gracious to others.

9. I will remember to negotiate. Negotiate. Negotiate.

10. I will be true to myself, my fiancé, and our vision.

11. Most importantly, I will have fun!

My Final Thought

Would you change your behavior if you were being reviewed?

One final thought. The *HuffPost* featured a blog basically suggesting what would happen if vendors could review brides and clients. I found this article to be fascinating because of how the integrity of vendors is always on the line and even more importantly their careers or entire business. The Internet, social media, and reviewer websites have made it all too easy for people to post their distaste about anything and everything. Whether it's fabricated or not, anyone can literally say anything they want. I'm not saying that all negative feedback is dramatized, but as the reader you're definitely only getting one side of the story. Plus, people in general are much more likely to write about the negative rather than focus or share their positive experiences, especially when it comes to weddings when emotions are running at an all-time high.

Unfortunately, that's just the way the world works. With that in mind, let's think about this for a minute. A review can literally destroy the reputation of one single person who has worked their entire life to get to where they are. Of course, if your photographer was two hours late and missed your ceremony, a bad review will be in their future.

However, if you are angry with them because they wouldn't hang from the ceiling so you could get a cool shot of you and your new spouse kissing upside down, he may not be in the wrong here. Ya see what I'm saying?

So, before you decide how to proceed and possibly share negative feedback with the world, think about what you're looking to gain. Money back? An apology? Or, are you intentionally looking to single-handedly take down one person.

The basis of the article was mainly asking would you act differently as a bride if a vendor could rate and review you. What if this one review could be seen by future or current employers? Colleagues? Friends and family? Would you have treated your vendors better? Honestly, would you have treated anyone and everyone around you better?

Would the feedback about you be negative or positive? I think you should definitely keep this in mind before becoming the next queen of writing reviews. Aspire to be the poised, elegant bride on the cover of *Martha Stewart Weddings*, not the horribly awful one featured on one of the network's biggest hit shows painting you in a not so favorable light.

I sincerely hope this book helps all you women out there getting engaged, already engaged, and knee deep in the planning process. I hope it helps to put things into perspective. Have fun and do not take everything so seriously! No matter what, it will all work out. It always does! Remember it really is *your* (and your fiancé's) day! So make it about the two of you and don't worry about what everyone else thinks!

Happy planning!

About the Author

What does Jessica bring to the table? With over 10 years of wedding-planning experience, Jessica Sclafini has not only planned hundreds of weddings, but she's probably stood-up in just as many. Jessica feels her knowledge of the wedding business can guide clients in the right direction. She's compiled a tremendous amount of helpful information that, at this point, has become second nature to her. Her tips will not only save the betrothed couple money, but will help them maintain their sanity along the way.

Oddly enough, Jessica has never been married. Growing-up in a large, very loud Italian family, however, has given her the strength to patiently deal with all different types of personalities: the good, the bad, and the crazy. Jessica can calm any irrational engaged couple.

She has been fortunate to build relationships with her clients that extend further than just the actual wedding, and has kept in touch with many through the years. Her honesty with a side of sarcasm and spiciness has been successful with her clients. She takes a very realistic approach throughout the process to not only keep brides grounded, but to help them remember what the day is truly about—the actual marriage and not just the party, which should always be fabulous!

So how does a single girl that never planned her own wedding, or even dreamt of being a bride as a kid, possibly becomes a wedding planner? "Glad you asked, I decided to throw myself into work after I left my family business and went through a terrible break up. So, clearly the obvious choice was to drown myself into planning other people's happily ever after. It's actually quite comical that I became a wedding planner. Planning a wedding in not about being the bride, it is about helping the bride execute her vision for the day that she has dreamed of since she was five with the ability to know where to cut costs and where to splurge. Being a wedding planner without ever being a bride should not make a difference, because it's a business and a career choice. So trust me, I can help plan your first...or second wedding"!

Made in the USA
Middletown, DE
27 November 2018